b r urned on or before
da

2

DAMAGE TO PAGES
P. 61-62
MISSING
NOTED
DATE: 15/11/00

Color in the Office

Color

Design Trends from 1950-1990

in the Office

and Beyond

Sara O. Marberry

Van Nostrand Reinhold
New York

Library of Congress Catalog Card Number 93-1363
ISBN 0-442-00944-5

I(T)P   Van Nostrand Reinhold is an International Thomson Publishing company.
ITP logo is a trademark under license.

Design by Patrick Seymour

Printed in Singapore

Van Nostrand Reinhold
115 Fifth Avenue
New York, NY 10003

International Thomson Publishing GmbH
Konigswinterer Str. 518
5300 Bonn 3
Germany

International Thomson Publishing
Berkshire House,168-173
High Holborn, London WC1V 7AA
England

International Thomson Publishing Asia
38 Kim Tian Rd., #0105
Kim Tian Plaza
Singapore 0316

Thomas Nelson Australia
102 Dodds Street
South Melbourne 3205
Victoria, Australia

International Thomson Publishing Japan
Kyowa Building, 3F
2-2-1 Hirakawacho
Chiyada-Ku, Tokyo 102
Japan

Nelson Canada
1120 Birchmount Road
Scarborough, Ontario
M1K 5G4, Canada

16 15 14 13 12 11 10 9 8 7 6 5 4 3 2 1

Library of Congress Cataloging-in-Publication Data

Marberry, Sara, 1959-
    Color in the office: design trends from 1950
to 1990 and beyond / Sara Marberry.
        p.   cm.
    Includes bibliographical references and index.
        ISBN 0-442-00944-5
        1. Office decoration—United States—History—20th century. 2. Color in
interior decoration. I. Title.
    NK2195.04M37 1993
    747'.94—dc20
                                        93-1363
                                        CIP

contents

a c k n o w l e d g m e n t s

The author wishes to thank the following people/organizations
for their help with and support for this book:

      Stanley Abercrombie, FAIA, *Interior Design* magazine

      Marvin Affrime, The Space Design Group

      Association of Contract Textiles

      Contract Design magazine

      Linda Folland, Herman Miller

      Neil Frankel, Perkins & Will

      Peter Jeff, Steelcase

      Richard Korsheen, ODA/Environetics

      Nancy Kwallek, Ph.D., University of Texas at Austin

      Cheryl Hurwitz, Stern & Associates

      Gregory Littleton, *Architecture* magazine

      Wayne Ruga

      Andre Staffelbach, Staffelbach & Associates

      Kristie Strassen

      Jenai Taylor, The Knoll Group

      Margaret Walch, Color Association of the U.S.

      Steve Yavrouian, Griswold, Heckel & Kelly

      Laurie Zagon

Special thanks to:

      Deborah Jaffe, for her thorough and professional
      research work.

      My husband, Richard, for his continued support,
      friendship, and love.

      Patrick Seymour, who designed this book.

preface

Very few ideas in this world are totally new; in fact, most ideas (which later turn into projects) are a result of seeing or hearing something that stimulates the brain and motivates one to develop it further. Such is the case with this book. The idea for it began with a lecture I heard by a member of the Color Marketing Group; it progressed into a lecture I developed to present as the "color" editor at *Contract* magazine; and it was transformed into a book after I left *Contract* in 1990 to pursue special projects.

Since I wasn't born until 1959, the history of color in the office before 1980 was not a subject that I could relate from personal experience. I had to rely on information gathered from interviews, magazine articles, and books; plus my own ability to interpret color and design trends of each decade. I am not a colorist; nor am I a designer. Rather, I am a journalist who has built up considerable knowledge about color and design. My expertise, therefore, lies in the ability to observe and write about trends.

Finding appropriate photos to document what I was writing about — especially from the '50s and '60s — was another challenge. I knew that many of the early commercial interior design firms no longer existed, and I discovered that most architecture and design firms have poor archives. Photos of early work have been lost, damaged, or lie unmarked in boxes in the storeroom. In addition, many noteworthy '50s office interiors were not even photographed in color! This is not unusual, since design magazines only published projects in black and white before the late '60s. Fortunately, descriptive captions were written to provide readers (and me) with an idea of the color scheme.

The quality of photography since the '50s has also changed most dramatically. As design became more advanced,

so did the practice of photography. So don't be disappointed if early office photos in this book lack clarity or depth — blame it on age and the technical prowess of the time.

Regionalism is another issue that was difficult to deal with. In the literature, color was treated as a broad issue; there were very few references to cultural or climatic differences. Perhaps this is a given: the light quality is definitely different in San Francisco than it is in New York; people in the midwest are different than those on the east coast or in the south, etc. Yet, color and design trends always mirror society, and the more sophisticated a society, the more complex its color palette. Because much of the published and referenced work in the '50s and '60s was from the east coast (New York City in particular, since that is where the design editors are located), it was hard for me to make or cite regional distinctions.

I should also mention that architects and interior designers were not responsible for choosing the color of office equipment. Obviously, this was handled by the client, who was at the mercy of the equipment manufacturers. As a result, early telephones and typewriters used in offices were primarily black, and computer hardware of the past 20 years has been consistently beige or "putty." Interestingly enough, the putty color of recent computer hardware has shifted from a yellow-based to a gray-based color, and some companies are even looking at offering other color options.

Finally, it is also a given that lighting design in office interiors did not come into its own until the late '70s and early '80s. Lighting is crucial to color rendition, and one of the main reasons that colors seem richer in the '80s and '90s is due to more sophisticated lighting techniques and equipment.

But this book is not about lighting. Nor is it about the experience of color, or making "proper" color choices to ensure the health and well-being of office workers (that is my next book). It is, quite simply, about the past, present, and future of color and design trends in the office.

Sara Marberry

Designers have no control over the color of office equipment. The most common colors in the past 20 years have been beige or putty.

PROJECT:

Coopers & Lybrand, Washington, D.C.

INTERIOR DESIGN:

Swanke Hayden Connell Architects.

PHOTO: *Maxwell McKenzie.*

introduction

As long as people have worked at something other than manual labor, there have been offices. According to *The Office Book*, the earliest office buildings were built in the 14th and 15th centuries for European governments, bankers, and barristers. Many homes in those times also functioned as an office or a store.

The Industrial Revolution of the late eighteenth and nineteenth centuries was the catalyst for the office to become a necessity for the control of operations. The first office building with a steel skeleton was built in 1884. Concurrently, the invention of the telegraph, telephone, and typewriter helped facilitate the workload and create thousands of clerking jobs. Usually desks were lined up on open floors, factory style, for control and efficiency. Daylight was the principal source of illumination.

It wasn't until after World War II that the technology for heating, ventilation, air conditioning, and lighting large interior spaces became cost-effective. Large corporate buildings began to shape America's urban landscape, a reflection of an expanding economy and a shift from an industrial focus to a service focus.

Nearly a half century later, office buildings have changed very little. Technology and access to information have altered the way people work, but the basic structure of the office building has remained the same. What has changed are the *interiors* of those offices — elements such as lighting, acoustics, furniture, fabrics, finishes, and space planning that reflect the shift from the office as a place to work to the office as the place to facilitate work.

Architecture has always influenced the design of offices, and it is architects who have had the most profound influence on color in the office. Perhaps the first visionary was Frank

Lloyd Wright. His designs for the Larkin Administration Building (1904) in Buffalo, N.Y., and Johnson Wax Company (1939) in Racine, Wis., were among the first to incorporate color schemes and provide large open spaces with natural light for workers. For Johnson Wax, Wright designed desks and chairs that were colored in the same rich earthy red as the brick on the outside of the building.

Yet prior to 1950, most offices were furnished with rows of green metal desks; with gray equipment, partitions, and file cabinets. Undoubtedly, many of the materials available today were hard to get or nonexistent back then. But, it wasn't until after World War II that a new world of possibilities opened up for manufacturing and design.

The basic truth is that although colors haven't really changed, the use of color in offices over the years has grown more sophisticated. Prior to 1980, architects and designers dealt with color in a monochromatic fashion, often using large expanses of color in a very graphic manner. True modernists didn't like to utilize color at all, except in the Bauhaus tradition of using primaries to make an architectural statement. After all, unlike a home or restaurant, the office was a serious place in which large numbers of people came to work. The rigid formula of the International Style did not allow for much diversity in office design.

One architect who challenged the bland, dehumanizing nature of the International Style and its influence on office design in the late '50s was Alexander Girard. Disappointed at the lack of choice in commercial fabrics, he created fabrics for Herman Miller that were spirited and colorful. Though still basically monochromatic, designers began to use more colors in the '60s, embracing a palette of avocado greens, burnt oranges, and turquoise blue. Yet, despite Girard's and others' efforts to change the status quo, the conservative nature of corporate America in the '50s, '60s, and much of the '70s called for tastefully restrained offices with few human touches.

In the '80s, companies got more aggressive, engaging in leveraged buyouts, corporate takeovers, and pushing their employees to 60-hour workweeks. The office became a second home for the ambitious executive. Companies started

Frank Lloyd Wright's forward-thinking design for the Larkin Administration Building in Buffalo, N.Y., in 1904 incorporated natural light and open space.

PHOTO: *Courtesy of the Buffalo and Erie County Historical Society.*

viewing their offices not as a physical amenity, but as a physical asset. Could the environment increase or decrease productivity? Probably. Hierarchies were out, team management was in.

Again, it was an architect who influenced the next change for color in office interiors. Although others had been touting the virtues of postmodern design for years, it was Michael Graves who brought it into the mainstream with his design for the Portland Administrative Services Building in 1981. Designers soon embraced the postmodern ornamentation and softer color palette. Gone was the monochromatic approach to color; in its place, sophisticated combinations of color, pattern, and materials were used to create visually rich environments.

So, much of what has influenced color and design in the American office in this century has been architecture. The Bauhaus founders laid the groundwork for the dominant style in the U.S. for almost 30 years. Wright, Girard, and Graves were architects who each had a different vision for interiors and for color. Architects Frank Gehry and Frank Israel are inspiring a new generation of architects to think differently about materials and color.

Yet, if the architects have been the inspiration for color and design in the office, interior designers have been the ones to refine the ideas and bring them down to a workable client level. After all, it is the client who ultimately approves the color and design scheme. The rigorous demands interior designers have made of lighting, textile, carpet, and furniture manufacturers have also contributed to breakthrough designs that have shaped the office landscape.

Extraordinary changes have occurred in America since 1950. When we look back at the offices over that time period, many may seem terribly unsophisticated and boring. But design is a process of learning — learning from the past and adapting to the present. If we can discover what influenced us, what facilitated change or new ideas, then we can proceed into the future with confidence.

Perhaps the first architect to
integrate exterior and interior colors in
the office, Wright chose shades
for secretarial desks and chairs that
matched the building materials of the 1939
Johnson Wax Building in Racine, Wis.

PHOTO: *Steelcase.*

the '50s
chapter one

World War II ended in 1945 and thus began the celebrated "Age of Affluence" in America. Driven by savings, it was the consumer's unspent overtime pay and industry's surplus profits that fueled the demand for new goods and services. *Life* magazine proclaimed in December 1959 that automated machines had "loosened a fresh windfall of inexpensive goods, many entirely new, to bring more comfort and enjoyment into daily life." With automation, Americans found themselves with more leisure time; the drudgery of many tasks was erased; and the shift from an industrial to a service society had begun.

As the cold war began, fear of communism contributed to increased defense spending by the U.S. Government. New home construction and public works expenditures were also key factors to America's economic expansion in the '50s. Consumer demand encouraged plant modernization and growth. Design and style consultant Christopher Pearce wrote that, "Conspicuous consumption was not only the foundation of mass production, it was also the main weapon in the Cold War." Prosperity was good for labor unions as well, as membership rose from 13 million to 17 million between 1946 and 1953. Higher costs compensated for the wage increases and "fringe" benefits negotiated by the unions.

As the Korean War was coming to a close in 1953, Dwight D. Eisenhower was elected president of the United States. Diplomacy advanced as 16 new countries were admitted to the United Nations in 1956, raising its total membership to 76. School segregation was abolished in 1954 and Rosa Parks touched off what would become almost two decades of racial strife by refusing to sit in the back of the bus in 1955.

TELEVISION TAKES OVER

While movies had been the primary entertainment of the '30s and '40s, television took over in the '50s. By 1957, 40 million American households had a TV. It had become a major social and political influence. "I Love Lucy," "Sgt. Bilko," "Dragnet," and "What's My Line?" were popular shows of the time. Hollywood countered by promoting the novelty of the big screen, introducing such innovations as 3-D viewing, stereophonic sound, and CinemaScope. *Sunset Boulevard* starring Gloria Swanson and William Holden was the hit of 1950; *On the Waterfront*, won a 1954 Oscar for its stars, Marlon Brando and Eva Marie Saint; and Marilyn Monroe surfaced to become the greatest sex symbol in the history of films. The cult of the teenager was also born in the '50s. Juvenile delinquency, epitomized by James Dean in the 1955 movie *Rebel Without a Cause*, rose — a result of youth trying to break away from conformity.

But conformity was a reality for most Americans in the '50s. Suburbia came into being as the number of cars between 1945 and 1955 doubled from 25 to 50 million. The station wagon became the preferred second car for grocery shopping. Americans were moving out of the cities to realize their dream of a house with brand new appliances, a two-car garage, and a yard — it didn't matter if it looked just like the one right next to it.

"The fifties, more than any period before, was the age when the design and furnishing of the home became an almost universal preoccupation, whether it was with designer articles or with the more mundane mass-produced items that nevertheless often attempted to capture the spirit of the modern look," wrote Pearce. The introduction of electric appliances liberated the housewife, and "by the end of the decade, the high-tech kitchen had become the universal ideal." Pink and aqua were the favorite "decor" colors, as new plastic materials and man-made fibers multiplied. Pink also became a favorite advertising color as new products were promoted with vigor.

Major exhibitions courted the consumer with "space age" technology and promises for the future. Products became streamlined. A main attraction of Disneyland, which opened in 1955, was "Tomorrowland." The rocket was a popular symbol of progress.

On the literary front, war novels and historical fiction were popular, while local symphony orchestras, art classes, and theatre groups multiplied. Classical music challenged jazz, and rhythm & blues filtered up from the South, where it as reborn as rock 'n' roll. In 1955, "Rock Around the Clock" became the first rock 'n' roll song to hit number one on the pop charts. Elvis Presley secured rock 'n' roll's future, and the more that parents complained about him, the more teenagers rebelled.

Fashion in the '50s was influenced by movie stars, country and western, swing, and rock 'n' roll music; and even the coronation of the Queen of England. Full skirts with waists and white gloves were considered sophisticated. Cosmetic jewelry, growing in popularity since the '40s, became a mainstay in the '50s with the advancement of plastics technology.

Chanel came back to fashion in 1954 with deceptively simple clothes designed for the working woman. A year later, Mary Quant made fashion headlines by recognizing the need for well-designed, affordable fashion that catered to the youthful market. Tube dresses, short shorts, and hats that could be purses were popular. Crisply styled Italian clothes for men, with narrow-cut jackets and trousers, were introduced to the fashion world in 1957, when John Stephen opened his first shop on Carnaby Street in London.

Better print technology and the development of synthetic fibers made leisurewear easier to design and produce, and styles became more casual. Du Pont introduced its "Dacron" polyester in the early '50s, but cotton enjoyed a revival at the end of the decade. Men wore Bermuda shorts and boys began to sport ducktail haircuts, blue jeans, black leather jackets, and white T-shirts. For girls, it was pastel-colored pedal pushers, turtlenecks, head scarves, and poodle skirts.

According to Pearce, "A new color sense emerged as synthetic dyes for use with both man-made and natural materials kept pace with developments in color photography, film, and paints."

ARCHITECTURE DOMINATED BY INTERNATIONAL STYLE

After World War II, the expanding American economy provided many opportunities to build. And, despite the trend of "Americanism," International Style architecture, with its European roots in the German Bauhaus movement, dominated commercial and residential construction in the '50s. Architects such as Marcel Breuer, Gordon Bunshaft, Walter Gropius, Phillip Johnson, Richard Neutra, and Mies van der Rohe rose to prominence by embracing this style.

Architectural historian Mary Hollingsworth wrote,

> "The International Style had developed out of an attempt to provide well-designed but low-cost housing, making a virtue out of the necessity for standardization. This virtue was exploited in the development of a style that had none of the pre-war socialist idealism but was motivated by the purely commercial need to provide maximum space at a minimum cost to gain maximum profit. The resulting buildings, with their industrial references to efficiency and organization, and lack of historical detail, were potent symbols for the new commercial age."

Characterized by open interiors, right angles, parallel lines, machine-like and unornamented precision, technical materials, and glass walls, International Style buildings became corporate America's symbol of "enlightened" capitalism in the '50s. As multinational companies consolidated and centralized operations, they commissioned high-rise office buildings in urban centers. Widespread use of air conditioning — a relatively new concept in the '50s — provided new interior comfort.

"We have to remember that the rise of the great corporations was enormously accelerated during the '50s and '60s, and there was presently a worldwide rash of 'image' buildings, mostly extruded towers of 40 to 100 stories, sheathed in stainless, aluminum, glass or precast sections, conspicuous monuments to the power and the enterprise of business,"

An electric blue wall provides color accent for a typical black, white, and gray general office area of the late '50s.

PROJECT:

Inland Steel, New York.

ARCHITECT/INTERIOR DESIGN:

Skidmore Owings & Merrill.

PHOTO: *Ezra Stoller, © ESTO.*

wrote furniture designer George Nelson in an introduction of a 1975 *Design Quarterly* issue on the design process at Herman Miller.

Interiors followed the design lead set by the buildings. Executive offices were appointed with modern furniture, area rugs, and artwork. It is interesting to note that during the early postwar years in America, the proper place for modern furniture was thought to be in the home. But good design and good quality furniture cost more than the general public could afford. According to Nelson, middle class America also rejected modern furniture "simply because the furniture wasn't fancy enough and did not weigh enough."

"These factors were not operative in the commercial market where a more favorable climate nudged the producers of good modern in the direction of contract business, and it was here that they found not only a market that could afford their wares, but their new spiritual home as well," he wrote.

Offices of the '50s were standardized and organized according to corporate hierarchy. General office spaces were laid out in very ordered form along wide corridors that were furnished with black or gray steel desks, resilient flooring, and steel partitions separating secretaries from the bosses' offices on the perimeter. Postwar era offices were typically cluttered until efficiently designed furniture-organized storage space began to appear in the '50s. Large lobbies signified status and prestige.

COMMERCIAL INTERIOR DESIGN AS A PROFESSION

Most commercial interiors in the '50s were done by architects instead of interior design specialists. "The architect found that he was being called in not only when a new structure was planned but also for remodeling and interior re-design," architect Caleb Hornbostel told *Architectural Record* in June 1952. But commercial interior design as a profession was beginning to hatch.

Under the direction of Florence Knoll, Knoll International's Planning Unit in New York City became a major force in office interior design in the '50s. A graduate of the Cranbrook Academy of Art in Bloomfield Hills, Mich., and the Architectural Association in London, she began doing

Light woods, sculpted chairs, and washed-out colors lend a Scandinavian feel to this late '50s "modern" executive office.
PROJECT:
Inland Steel, New York.
ARCHITECT/INTERIOR DESIGN:
Skidmore Owings & Merrill.
PHOTO: *Ezra Stoller, © ESTO.*

When used with white or black, primary colors were considered acceptable to Modernist architects. Note the full-height temporary partitions and grid of fluorescent lights.
PROJECT:
Inland Steel, Chicago, IL.
ARCHITECT/INTERIOR DESIGN:
Skidmore Owings & Merrill.
PHOTO: *Hedrich-Blessing, courtesy Chicago Historical Society.*

commercial interior space planning and design as early as 1943.

"Prior to World War II, most nonresidential interiors were either designed by the architects for the buildings or were not designed at all," she wrote in 1964. "More often than not, the building itself was at violent odds with its interior requirements: while the structure might be neoclassical, the functional requirements of the interiors were frequently modern in the extreme, so that either the interior spaces would match the exterior (and thus not at all), or they would be made to function reasonably well — in which case the furnishings were not likely to match the style of the building."

"This inherent conflict," she continued, "was resolved by a number of pioneer architects in the early part of the 20th century . . . [who] designed and built commercial and industrial structures in which exterior form and interior space were completely integrated, and both served the needs of 20th century building programs. To achieve this . . . [they] discovered that they had to design the furniture as well as the actual building. As a result, almost all the really significant, early innovations in modern furniture design were carried out by architects. . . The reason these architects had to design their own interiors down to lighting fixtures and doorknobs was obvious: the 'interior decorators' of the time had no knowledge of modern architecture — or, if they had, they were generally out of sympathy with it."

Florence Knoll revolutionized the process of interior design by analyzing the client's requirements to offer a synthesis of space, furniture, mechanical equipment, color and fabric, art, graphics, and finishing details. A major force in interior design, she developed a trademark style that became the blueprint for contemporary office furnishings an interiors.

One of Florence Knoll's colleagues in the Planning Unit in the '40s was Davis Allen, who joined Skidmore Owings & Merrill (SOM) in 1950 as a junior architectural designer. His elegant, though cool, modern interiors for SOM clients also helped establish the integrated approach to corporate interior design in the '50s.

In *The Office Book,* author Judy Graf Klein states that Union Carbide, completed in 1959 by the New York office of

Red accessories accent a late '50s brochure
photo of Steelcase's Flight Line
Sabre desk, shown in charcoal and silver gray
finish with silver gray Textolite tops.
PHOTO: *Steelcase.*

SOM, is recognized by many to be the first building with totally integrated interiors. Designed by Jack Dunbar, an associate partner in the firm, Union Carbide's interiors featured a visual harmony between ceilings, partitions, and filing cabinets. The modular design lined partitions up with exterior window mullions.

Founded in the late 1940s, Designs for Business in New York was another early pioneer in commercial interiors. Director of Design Gerald Luss has been credited with influencing the design of metal casework and moveable partitions in several manufacturer's standard lines. Michael Saphier, who later went on to found Saphier Lerner Schindler (SLS) with Larry Lerner and Bud Schindler, also had a design

practice in the '50s. Labeled by some as "the college of interior design," many talented interior designers who went on to establish their own practices in the '60s began their careers with SLS.

Maria Bergson, who established her New York design practice in 1945, was one of the few independent commercial interior designers in the '50s. Specializing in the design of offices, banks, hotels, hospitals, stores, and other commercial interiors, she also designed accompanying furniture and lighting fixtures.

Upon her induction into its Hall of Fame in 1990, *Interior Design* magazine stated in its December issue, "As early as 1949 she devised 64-sq. ft. partitioned modular work stations that provided a maximum of work surface within arm's reach. At the same time, she began to suspect that executives took three-hour lunches in order to relax, and that comfortable, well-appointed offices could get them back to work more quickly. By comfortable, she meant designed specifically for business, not simply plucked out of a residential line likely to be too downy soft. . . ."

OFFICE FURNITURE GOES MODERN

As America embraced modernism, Herman Miller and Knoll began designing contemporary office furniture in the '40s. Other large companies, such as Steelcase and General Fireproofing, were also producing office furniture at that time, but it was more along the lines of mass-market gray metal desks. Although Art Metal was responsible for taking the desk designed by SOM's Davis Allen into production, both Herman Miller and Knoll were unique in that they employed architects or designers with interior planning experience who brought a new perspective to furniture style.

"Florence Schust [Knoll] did not think of herself then as a furniture designer but rather as a designer of interiors with opinions about furniture," wrote Eric Larabee in *Knoll Design*. "The early days were hard. Not only was it difficult to get work involving contemporary designs, but after a client and a job had been found it was still difficult to produce the product. . . . The only available material was wood and even the available glues to hold it together were inferior. . . ."

Red was one of Florence Knoll's "signature" colors in the interiors work she pioneered through the Planning Unit at Knoll.

PHOTO: *The Knoll Archives.*

In 1953, Steelcase introduced "Sunshine Styling," the office furniture industry's first desks in distinctive colors patterned after desert scenes.

PHOTO: *Steelcase.*

George Nelson is credited with introducing architectural detailing and color into desks for Herman Miller in 1958. Unfortunately, the line was too costly to produce.

PHOTO: *Herman Miller.*

In March 1946, *Interiors* magazine described Knoll's Planning Unit as "a proving ground for a group of young designers with architectural and engineering background, who refuse to compromise with the taste of a dictatorial public. A loose collaborative arrangement has benefited both designers and manufacturer." Included in that group were Jens Risom, Abel Sorenson, Ralph Rapson, Eero Saarinen, and George Nakashima, who were, of course, headed by Florence Knoll.

Typical construction materials for many of Florence Knoll's furniture designs of the '50s included teak, rosewood, marble, and polished steel — most often accented by brightly colored fabric in "Knoll red" or cobalt blue.

Yet, just as Knoll was taking New York by storm, Herman Miller had quietly assembled its own stable of talented designers in Western Michigan. Gilbert Rohde, a display illustrator from the advertising industry, approached the company in 1930 with ideas for modern furniture designs. His modular office furniture and storage system, the Executive Office Group introduced in 1942, had 15 components that could be arranged in approximately 400 different combinations. Rohde's furniture was simple and often neutral in color. Comprised of wood veneer with black metal and chrome legs, the Executive Office Group was a perfect compliment to the International Style interior.

Even though Steelcase had introduced color options for desks in 1953, it is George Nelson at Herman Miller who is credited with the idea of including architectural detailing and color in desks. An architect by training, Nelson was an editor at *Architectural Forum* in 1945 when he was approached by D.J. DePree, the founder and head of Herman Miller, after reading an article by Nelson titled, "Storagewall," about a revolutionary idea for storage components based on interchanging furniture with architectural elements. The design genesis for open plan furniture systems that dominate offices of today, Storagewall was the first of many products that Nelson would design for the company over the next 20 years.

Nelson's Modern Management Group, introduced in 1958, featured desks and returns made of wood, steel, and Micarta in mustard, cobalt blue, and orange colors. Unfortunately, the line was too costly for Herman Miller to

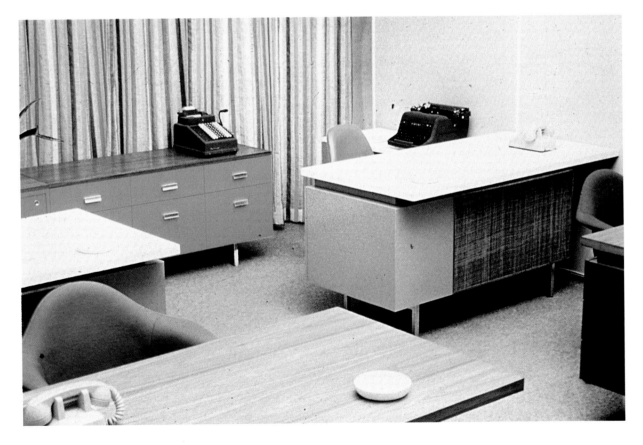

produce and it was soon dropped. "But the principle of including architectural detailing and color into desks was correct," D.J. DePree told Ralph Caplan in 1976, "and it was proven correct by Steelcase, General Fireproofing, and others. We had failed to make the product accessible to the marketplace, but George made a tremendous contribution to the steel furniture industry."

Other industrial designs in the '40s and '50s reflected the exuberant, rounded, abstract style called biomorphism, which was inspired by the work of painters Pablo Picasso and Joan Miro and sculptors Hans Arp and Alexander Calder. Isamu Noguchi's kidney-shaped tables and Charles Eames's potato-chip chairs for Herman Miller came out of this movement, as well as other interpretations by architects and designers for dinnerware, glassware, and jewelry. As a style it was interesting, but was more appropriate for residential interiors than the office.

TEXTILE INNOVATORS

Although textile companies such as Boris Kroll, Lee Jofa/Groundworks, Ben Rose, Maharam/Vertical Surfaces, Scalamandre, and F. Schumacher were established before 1950, prior to that time most fabrics used for commercial installations were either privately commissioned custom orders or designs selected from residential collections. According to the Association of Contract Textiles (ACT) it was not until the early '50s that textile companies began to design, stock, and market products specifically for commercial applications. "The majority of these fabrics were simple piece-dyed plain weaves. The typical palette consisted of basic reds, greens, yellows, and blues enhanced by natural colors," wrote ACT in 1990.

After World War II, there was a demand for printed and woven fabric designs that would work with contemporary furniture designs and architecture. According to *American Fabrics*, patterns became more architectural with "brilliant colors and bold motifs — line silhouetted against mass, weight equalized with color."

Although textiles were used as "art" and hung much like tapestries in many office interiors, the bold design direction

Alexander Girard's love of color and pattern set a new direction for contract textiles in the '50s. The floral pattern, "Mikado," was introduced in 1954 (opp. page top), and "Crosses" came out in 1957 (opp. page bottom).

PHOTOS: *Herman Miller.*

described by *American Fabrics* was probably more true for residential fabrics than for those used in commercial spaces. "By the 1950s and sixties, most textiles used in public spaces were devoid of color and pattern and, in some circles, were strongly condemned for their lack of human feeling. Critics complained that these fabrics were so devoted to functionalism that they had lost their appeal to the senses of sight and touch," wrote Ann Erickson and Delores Ginthner with Jo Ann Undem for Herman Miller in 1985.

That changed when Alexander Girard, whose love of pattern and color set a new direction for commercial textiles in the '50s. A respected architect who started his practice in Grosse Pointe, Mich., and later moved to Santa Fe, N.M., Girard had gained recognition in the 1940s for his designs of homes and commercial interiors in the Detroit area. He was a color consultant to the GM Research Center from 1951-52 and served as design director of Herman Miller's Textile Division from 1952-68.

Under his direction, Herman Miller introduced fabrics for office interiors that "used brilliant, primary colors in a bold, exciting way that completely broke with tradition." He wanted a full spectrum of color choices for commercial fabrics.

Girard's strong colors and geometric patterns introduced a joyful, warm spirit into commercial textiles. "The simple geometric patterns and brilliant primary color ranges came to be because of my own urgent need for them on current projects," he was quoted as saying in a 1975 issue of *Design Quarterly*. According to textile designer Jack Lenor Larsen, who wrote the essay on Girard in that same publication, he was "one of the great colorists, pattern givers, environmental and exhibition designers of our time." (Larsen's company, founded in 1952, was also an early textile innovator, though mostly with residential fabrics.)

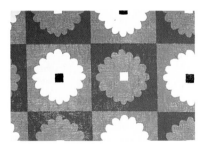

Besides Girard, the textile designs of Dorothy Liebes and Jim Thompson offered a new color sensibility in the '50s. "All three popularized vibrant, pulsating color by making it available in fabric form," wrote Larsen. "Although Girard's concern is the deepest, broadest and most durable, he shares with Liebes and Thompson a keen interest in ethnic

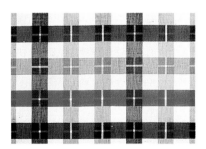

expression and in infusing American culture with the spice of an exotic expansiveness."

Larsen also pointed out that the three designers' interest and background in architecture led them to be more concerned with fabric color and texture rather than structure. "If Girard had ever devoted himself to the complexities of fabric construction he undoubtedly would have dwarfed us all," he wrote.

Knoll created its textile division in 1947, which was headed by Arundell Clarke. Eszter Haraszty succeeded her in 1949. A Hungarian emigré, Haraszty was reported to be a "brilliant colorist" with a flamboyant character. After the Planning Unit had done its preliminary work, Haraszty chose the colors, often using orange and pink. According to Larsen, she and Evelyn Hill worked with Rancocas to "give Knoll an extraordinary upholstery collection of wools mixed with nylon monofilaments in the colors of peacocks and persimmons." She was responsible for two of the company's most famous designs, "Knoll Stripe," and the industrial-strength "Transportation Cloth."

COLOR AS ACCENT

In keeping with the philosophy of the Bauhaus founders, International Style architects and designers used color to emphasize form, rather than simply as decoration. Purists favored black and white interiors. But others recognized that bold colors could compliment this ideology, utilizing primary colors against black, white, and gray for architectural effect. Perhaps they also recognized that strict International Style interiors, while sophisticated, tended to be cold and impersonal. As early as 1954, *Progressive Architecture* reported in its December issue that the "business-like look has given way to colorful interiors with almost a home-like atmosphere." The magazine also asserted that, "For over-all appearance, unbroken planes of color and texture are more effective and conducive to work than many unrelated divisions of space."

Intense yellows, red-oranges, greens, and cobalt blues began to contrast with the International Style palette of white, light gray, and black in many office interiors. A popular technique was to paint one wall of a private office with an accent color. As salmon, sea foam, and hot pink were finding their way into the home, beige and brown were used to bring the residential feel into the office.

For Connecticut General Life Insurance Company's executive offices in Hartford, the Knoll Planning Unit executed what has come to be known as its "signature" approach — a neutral palette accented with brilliant color. Materials of choice were polished chrome and stainless steel; hand woven silks, linens, wools; wax-finished teak and walnut; and travertine and Carrara marble.

The color scheme for H.M.H. Publishing Company in Chicago, designed by Ralph Stoetzel, Architect, was described by *Progressive Architecture* in January 1958 as "Very light or very dark colors set off by accent notes of vivid orange, olive, black, and white. Orange, used for one wall in reception area, is separated in upholstery, cabinet doors, and other spots throughout all offices."

Always one of the most popular colors, blue was one of the major colors used by the U.N. Planning Office in the early '50s for the United Nations Secretariat office in New York City. The U.N. interiors also featured three shades of gray — a "military" palette that became the trademark of many government buildings.

But some designers were experimenting with softer colors in the '50s. Interior designer Eleanor Le Maire used "light, atmospheric colors — sea foam, willow, blue smoke, cloud blue, and sun yellow" in the design of an office reception area in New York City in the mid-'50s, which was published in *Progressive Architecture* in December 1954.

So, as the '50s came to a close, office interiors were beginning to show more complex designs, patterns, and colors. Technology was advancing and living in the modern age was no longer such a great phenomenon. Americans were traveling abroad, bringing back a more eclectic sense of style. The country was prospering; families were secure; the dream was coming true. And the '60s were just around the corner.

the '60s
chapter two

Many have described the '60s as the decade of tumult and change. Indeed, what happened in the '60s transformed America's social and cultural foundation and profoundly influenced the character of the '70s, if not the '80s and '90s. But the '60s didn't start out rough. In a review of the decade in December 1969, *Life* magazine divided the '60s into two parts, citing a feeling of hope and optimism in the first half that shifted to demands for extreme change after 1965.

In his inaugural address in 1960, President John Fitzgerald Kennedy urged people to share the burdens of leadership. His idealism appealed to America's youth, the optimistic baby boomers who had an urgent stake in the quality of life. Americans were eager for heroes, and John Glenn became one when he orbited the Earth three times in 1962. The post-World War II expansion had created a thriving world economy and the future looked bright.

But there was an undercurrent of change. Martin Luther King gave his famous "I have a dream" speech to over 200,000 who marched on Washington in 1963. Then, on November 22, 1963, President Kennedy was shot and killed while riding in an open automobile through the streets of Dallas. Americans were shocked, saddened, and the sense of disillusionment began.

Under new President Lyndon B. Johnson's direction, the war in Vietnam soon escalated. The Civil Rights Act was passed in 1964, but according to *Life*, the sudden and violent Watts

Riots in Los Angeles in August 1965 was the turning point that "set the tone of confrontation and open revolt" that dominated the latter part of the decade.

Anti-war protests on college campuses and race riots in America's inner cities soon became commonplace. Students established a "generation gap" with their elders by embracing the drug culture and rock music that fueled its frenetic highs. The Beatles, the Doors, and the Rolling Stones ascended to rock "superstardom" during this era. Bob Dylan and Joan Baez sang troubled tales of social protest, nonviolence, and love that were the anthems of America's youth.

THE "ANYTHING GOES" ERA

So-called "mainstream" culture was also affected by this attitude of change. "New experience soon became the order of the day," wrote *Life* editors. "The stage, the screen, the arts, the fashions, all offered innumerable fresh possibilities for shock and confrontation."

Indeed, the '60s saw the introduction of the topless bathing suit, miniskirt, hip-hugging bell bottom pants with wide belts, body suits, and fishnet stockings. Suit lapels became wider, as did neckties. Bright colors and strong patterns were part of the "anything is in" philosophy of the '60s. Fashion imitated fine art as designers interpreted the geometric patterns and primary colors of Piet Mondrian in their work. The Beatles brought the "mod" look to America in 1964 with their crisp suits and "bowl" haircuts, but soon were sporting longer locks and "hippie" clothes inspired by Middle Eastern kaftans, beads, and headbands. Body painting and theatrical fashion became an art, and hemlines dropped to midi length at the end of the decade.

Pop art, which originated in London in the '50s, startled Americans in the '60s through fresh interpretations by artists such as Andy Warhol, Jasper Johns, David Hockney, and Roy Lichtenstein. Using everyday images, such as Coke bottles, Campbell's Soup cans, and Brillo boxes, Warhol mocked modern consumer society. Lichtenstein exploited comic strips as a medium. Op art, consisting of undulating geometric patterns that created optical illusions, was short-lived, but yet another expression of the bizarre.

On Broadway, *Hair* became the first rock musical to earn mainstream success. In Hollywood, producers were churning out Westerns, but also dealing with racial issues, as in Sidney Poitier's portrayal of a big city black detective who helps a Southern sheriff in *In the Heat of the Night* and as a black man who wants to marry a middle-class white woman in *Guess Who's Coming to Dinner* in 1967. Two different pictures of America's youth were painted in Dustin Hoffman's 1967 portrayal of a naive middle-class college kid in *The Graduate*; and the motorcycling, dope-smoking alienated youth played in 1969 by Peter Fonda and Dennis Hopper in *Easy Rider*.

Through television, Americans saw men walk on the moon, heard about the killings of Robert Kennedy and Martin Luther King in graphic detail, and saw gruesome images of the Vietnam War. Hippy humor was expressed by the comedy show, "Laugh In" in 1967. Other comedy dramas, such as "I Dream of Jeannie," "Bewitched," and "Batman" were also popular. "I Spy" and "Mission Impossible" echoed America's fascination with the cold war; and the short-running, but successful "Star Trek" explored the frontiers of space.

Meanwhile, the "space race" had speeded up America's technological breakthroughs. The first work on ergonomics was done for U.S. tanks, but stimulated by the needs of men in space. Teflon was used on spacecraft and later patented by Du Pont for cookware. The first desktop computer was introduced by Olivetti in 1966, and by 1969, IBM had introduced the first network to link desktop hardware. Medical science had advanced considerably, developing the first artificial heart pump and kidney in 1960, but it wasn't until 1969 that the first successful kidney transplant was completed. The first Japanese car, the Toyota Corona, was sold in the U.S. in 1965.

MODERNISM REACHES NEW HEIGHTS

Architectural firms grew by leaps and bounds in the '60s, as America's cities continued to embrace the International Style or "modernist" tradition. Concrete, glass, and steel buildings provided the most cost-effective and efficient means of housing the growing number of white collar workers. "Manacled by the economic need to cram ever more people onto the limited real estate of Manhattan island, most architects [in the '60s] were forced to design what amounted to towering file cabinets," *Life* magazine observed in 1969. Giant skyscrapers, such as SOM's John Hancock Center in Chicago and Walter Gropius's Pan Am Building in New York emerged as symbols of success and power for huge multinational corporations.

Yet despite its enormous popularity, architects began to question modernism in the '60s. In 1962, the terminal Eero Saarinen designed for TWA at New York's Kennedy Airport was made of concrete, glass, and steel, and shaped like an eagle in flight. Believing that the humorless functionalism of the modernists belonged to the 1930s, Philadelphia architect Robert Venturi proclaimed "less is a bore" in his 1966 book, *Complexity and Contradiction in Architecture*. He urged architects to borrow from other styles — even Las Vegas pop art. Paul Rudolph, Louis Kahn, and Le Corbusier pioneered "brutalist" architecture in the '60s, treating buildings as expressionistic sculptures with heavy geometric forms.

Architectural historian Mary Hollingsworth observes that this questioning of modernism coincided with the deaths of four leading twentieth century architects: Frank Lloyd Wright in 1959; Le Corbusier in 1965; and Mies van der Rohe and Walter Gropius in 1969. Nevertheless, opposition to modernism did not gain full steam until the '70s.

EMERGENCE OF CONTRACT DESIGN FIRMS

By the late '50s, the word "contract" was coined as a word for commercial interior design. *Contract*, the first trade magazine exclusively devoted to covering contract furnishings began publication in November 1960. In a statement to readers, the publishers explained that they had "become aware of the lack of a medium specifically devoted to the affairs of the contract furnishings industry. The immediate occasion for this flash of insight was the January 1958 winter furniture market in Chicago, where a surprising number of manufacturers turned up, many of them for the first time, with "contract lines."

Interior design firms that eventually became industry giants, such as Gensler and Associates, Griswold Heckel & Kelly, and I S D were founded in the '60s. Faced with new

competition, Knoll's Planning Unit continued to do interiors, but its influence waned, especially without the leadership of Florence Knoll, who retired in 1965.

No longer the sole domain of the architect, contract interior designers quickly established an expertise in office design. Color, materials, and selection of furniture were standard requirements, but the emergence of electronic data processing machines in the work place soon made space planning, acoustics, and lighting just as important.

Advances in construction techniques and methodology, as well as improved fluorescent lighting, made large interior office spaces possible. The grid approach favored by International Style architects remained dominant, with executive and management offices usually located on the perimeter and lobby areas serving as signature spaces. Flexibility concerns prompted designers to create moveable partitions, which later became part of manufacturers' standard lines.

General office area with red, yellow, and blue accents is the picture of crisp efficiency. Note the wide hallways and temporary full-height partitions.

PROJECT:

Unidentified.

INTERIOR DESIGN:

Griswold, Heckel & Kelly Associates Inc. (GHK).

PHOTO: *GHK.*

In the mid-'60s, some challenged the idea of locating executives next to the windowed perimeter and began to provide better spaces for the clerical staff. Use of translucent glass partitions were frequently used to admit daylight into central office spaces. Commenting on the "lamentable sameness" in general office areas, John Anderson wrote in *Contract* magazine in 1963: "This is especially true in the new glass skyscrapers, where it is rare indeed to find desks and cabinets in anything else but the slim metal frames and thin plastic or wood tops and pedestals in what might be called the SOM style. . . ."

Dissatisfied with the furniture offered for the office market, many architects and designers created their own, which was later put into production by manufacturers. Despite the proliferation of the "SOM style" metal desk, executive wood desk groupings became popular in the mid-'60s. Imported designs from Finland, Sweden, Switzerland, and Italy encouraged a new design aesthetic for the office as well.

Designers in the '60s were also promoting the use of artwork and graphics to provide visual interest, color, and a corporate statement of quality. "Art in Offices . . . The Study of the Space that Surrounds Us," an exhibit at the Corcoran Gallery in Washington, D.C., in 1966, featured vignettes designed by Barbara R. Weiner that showed how art, color, and appealing furniture could be used to make a personal statement. "The typical office environment is impersonal and anonymous. It is without color, design, or form," Weiner was quoted as saying in *Contract* magazine in 1966. "It is bland, stereotyped, and neutral. It lacks interest. Into this impersonal and anonymous environment we plot a human being. He often reacts with profound indifference."

TEXTILE DIRECTIONS

Throughout the '50s and into the '60s, the use of window hangings to cover large areas of glass in contemporary buildings had become commonplace. Casements — fabrics that appeared flat and opaque from the outside, but were patterned on the inside — were developed to provide interior visual interest while preserving the neutral facade of buildings.

Light woods, gold, turquoise, and pastel shades reflect the Scandinavian influence of this early '60s office interior. Architecturally "sculpted" ceilings in the reception area are painted in different colors; they house fluorescent lighting in the conference room.

PROJECT:

Sterling Drug, New York.

INTERIOR DESIGN:

Griswold, Heckel & Kelly Associates Inc.

(GHK).

PHOTOS: *GHK.*

In 1961, *American Fabrics* magazine criticized the "glass-walled canyon of New York's Park Avenue" office buildings as being devoid of color or pattern, citing them as "carefully controlled interiors" that "lack the human touch." The editors admitted that there was textile beauty in these interiors, but in such a pure form that it was "lost to the senses." They observed that the dominant textile colors were white, off-white, or natural. The reasons for this were because architects and interior designers felt that textiles should not distract from other elements of design (artwork, wall colors); printed fabrics became quickly outdated and with such large areas of glass to cover, were expensive to replace; and printed and dyed textiles were not yet fade-proof to withstand glare.

"I am for true color . . ." wrote Florence Knoll in the same article, "true neutrals and true bright colors. Patterned textile can be used in interiors, but they must be used sparingly. Because they are more distracting than solid colors, they have a tendency to become monotonous when seen day after day."

Acknowledging a trend toward more decoration and use of printed textiles, the editors pointed to an expanding role for textiles on walls, and as tapestries — which could be regarded as artwork, providing a "point of brilliant color interest in an otherwise 'undecorated' interior."

For upholstery, the widespread use of fabric finishing and the development of vinyl and other synthetic textiles brought a greater range of color choices for contract designers in the '60s.

According to ACT, the free spirit of the late '60s was a powerful influence on contract textiles. "Psychedelic brights and Op Art graphics found their way into fabric design," the association observed in 1990, citing the work of Ben Rose and Boris Kroll. "Big bold patterns gained a foothold where pattern had been non-existent. Strong, bright colors and combinations such as fuchsia and orange or bright green and blue were the order of the day."

BRIGHT COLORS AND MONOCHROMATIC DESIGN

In 1960, color authority Faber Birren wrote in *Contract* magazine, "Color for the sake of color is hardly sufficient." He urged designers to appraise color in both functional and human preference terms; and to use it to improve illumination, reduce glare, lessen visual and physical fatigue, and give a sense of comfort and pleasure. Birren warned against using bright colors, as they would distract workers from their tasks.

"Where workplaces are concerned, simplicity is the keynote. Soft colors, which lack distraction, are modified in tone and get less dirty than clean colors," he wrote. "It is also more economical practice to use white for all ceilings and one trim color throughout a building. . . ." His "functional palette" for working environments included white (for ceilings), soft pale blue-green, light green, pink/coral, pale yellow, light gray, and medium gray (for trim).

Although contract designers may have been aware of Birren's research, they did not necessarily heed his advice. The revolt against "textile purity" predicted by *American Fabrics* magazine began to appear in office designs of the early '60s, which show widespread use of bright primary colors, generally in upholstery or carpets. Set against beige, gray, and brown-black neutrals of modernism, red-orange, bright "avocado" green, mustard yellow, and royal blue seemed to be the palette of choice. Use of color in upholstery and carpet was very monochromatic, but designers weren't afraid to combine many colors into one space.

For example, an executive office in New York designed by Becker and Becker, published by *Interiors* magazine in 1960, boasted a walnut ceiling panel; moss green carpet; white walls; flame leather-covered armchairs; a sofa in gold yellow, orange, and brown striped fabric; gold vinyl wallcovering; and pumpkin-colored chair upholstery fabric. Another project designed by Peter Fraiser, in the same issue, was cited for its "deft use of sculptural curves, vivid colors, and modern furnishings to give . . . [the office] a contemporary air with Victorian overtones." The chairman's office featured red and purple Knoll pedestal chairs, a mustard wallcovering, and gold carpeting.

Yet, there still were some modernist purists in the early '60s. "Spartan elegance" was how *Progressive Architecture* described the president of Maritime Overseas Corporation's New York office in an article it published in 1963. Interior

Called out of retirement to complete the
interiors for CBS, Florence Knoll
placed primary colors against rich woods
in one executive office (left).

PROJECT:

CBS, New York.

ARCHITECT:

Eero Saarinen.

INTERIOR DESIGN:

Florence Knoll.

PHOTO: *Knoll Archives.*

designers Designs for Business used white walls, natural textures, teak floors, marble tops, and a metal telephone bracket to create refinements in design that were still well within the realm of the staid and stern modernist tradition. Multicolored files were the only accent in the predominately white general office and accounting space.

A secretarial area designed for the Eastern Regional Offices of Eastman Kodak by The Space Design Group was described as "airy and cheerful" by *Interiors* in 1964. Its white background was offset by walls covered in bright green, yellow, or orange fabric; and secretarial chairs in yellow-orange upholstery.

Florence Knoll was called out of retirement to finish interiors for the new CBS building in New York, at the death of its architect, Eero Saarinen, in 1961. Considered to be a "brilliant exit for a brilliant career," Knoll's design for executive offices featured dark bronze carpeting and beige walls to provide a background for CBS's collection of painting and sculpture. Although liberal in its use of red and yellow, CBS was one of the first projects in which Knoll broke away from the basic primaries to experiment with more subtle shades.

Bold colors on Knoll "Pollock" chairs
liven up this reception area of the late '60s.
PROJECT:
House of Studies, Ohio Dominican College,
Columbus, OH.
INTERIOR DESIGN:
Design Collective Incorporated.
PHOTO: *Design Collective Incorporated.*

Sixties "kitsch" personifies this
executive office. Dark wood, black leather, and
chrome contrasts with white
travertine, white leather, white upholstery,
white plastic tables, an electric blue
area rug, and colorful hanging objects.
PROJECT:
Unidentified.
INTERIOR DESIGN:
Griswold, Heckel & Kelly Associates, Inc.
(GHK).
PHOTO: *GHK.*

Supergraphics, a trend in the late '60s and
early '70s, liven up this stark interior corridor
space for a Manhattan ad agency (opp. page).
PROJECT:
Benton & Bowles, New York.
INTERIOR DESIGN:
The Space Design Group.
PHOTO: *Bernard Liebman.*

"BOLD NEW POLY-EXPANDED MEGA-DECORATION"

Progressive Architecture (PA) observed that in the early
'60s, ". . . architects and designers dreamed of pure, clean,
off-white-and-beige, rectilinear interiors — crisply defined
with machine-age stainless steel furniture and enriched by
organic, natural-grown textures in deep wools and burl woods.
A tentative, romantic use of materials and of surprising can-
tilevers, and an occasional re-analysis of functions were also
apparent, but above all, 'tastefulness' was the goal."

Consistent in approach, even
forgotten corners were given color
and graphic treatment (left).

PROJECT:

Benton & Bowles, New York.

INTERIOR DESIGN:

The Space Design Group.

PHOTO: *Bernard Liebman.*

Colored panels and parquet flooring

distinguish this early '60s corridor.

PROJECT:

Eastman Kodak, New York.

INTERIOR DESIGN:

The Space Design Group.

PHOTO: *Bernard Liebman.*

Proclaiming a revolution in 1968, *PA*'s editors cited the emergence, as early as 1965, of a new breed of architect and interior designer, whose approach "shows a bold, energized new look derived from a reacceptance of decoration within the vocabulary of architectural design. . . . The new decoration manifests attitudes of perverse trickery (both optical and intellectual), devices of explosive scale (transparency, reflectiveness, and simultaneity), and the permissive superimposition of chaos onto existing 'tasteful' spaces. It is Mega-Decoration."

In terms of color, the most obvious trend resulting from the Mega-Decoration phenomenon was the advent of "supergraphics" in office interiors. Large scale geometric forms — often diagonal — in bright, primary colors energized walls and floors. It was color for color's sake — a charged-up interior for the "electric" age. Created with paint, or through carpet and fabric designs on floors or walls, supergraphics was another device designers used to alter the scale of traditional rectilinear interiors.

Artwork and hidden screen show uniform

graphic approach to color and design. Avocado

green, a late '50s holdover color, had staying

power through the '60s (opp. page bottom).

PROJECT:

Benton & Bowles, New York.

INTERIOR DESIGN:

The Space Design Group.

PHOTO: *Bernard Liebman.*

Perhaps a reflection of the tumultuous times, this new approach to interiors was a rebellion against the strict modernist dogma of the past 15-20 years that were challenged in the '60s by the writings and work of architects Robert Venturi and Charles Moore. But perhaps, more significantly, the new approach brought with it a new awareness of the physical and psychological needs of people through, as *PA* described it, "expanded flexibility in the functional orientation of objects."

OFFICE LANDSCAPE

This new awareness of the needs of people and the desire to create visual chaos as a design goal was exemplified in the principles of open office landscape. Originated in Germany by the Quickborner Team in the early '60s, this new phenomenon in office planning was introduced to the U.S. in 1964.

Controversial because it did away with private offices and put people out in an open floor, office landscape was

based on the principle that the office layout should reflect the work process. People were positioned according to traffic flow; traditional desks were replaced with tables; walls were replaced with partitions; and files were removed to file rooms. It was markedly different from the rectangular-plan partitioning systems that were the hallmark of office design in the late '50s and early '60s.

The first office landscape in the U.S. was designed by the Quickborner Team in 1967 for the Freon Division of E.I. Du Pont de Nemours & Company in Wilmington, Del. Intended to be an experiment, Du Pont managers were impressed by improved communication among staff members and were pleased with the flexibility of the system to accommodate change.

Because it required upholstered panels, carpeting, and window coverings to absorb noise created by its open areas, office landscaping also encouraged the use of color. It gave impetus to the panel fabrics and commercial carpet industries, whose manufacturers and suppliers soon began to experiment with new patterns and colors. However, it would be a while before sophisticated texture and color combinations would appear in textiles and carpet — although bold, color use in the office was still basically monochromatic.

Meanwhile, convinced that office furniture design had gone as far as it could in terms of aesthetic refinement, Herman Miller recruited Robert Probst in the early '60s to work with George Nelson to develop a new system. Probst agreed with the Quickborner Team's idea that offices should be responsive, and his first designs in 1964 featured desks, communication/telephone booths, and storage bins that were either supported by aluminum legs/pedestals or on a wall track.

Designed to integrate color with wood and polished aluminum, furniture components featured a rounded profile with desktops that could be either flat or slanted. End panels were made of molded plastic and available in olive green, electric blue, dark blue, black, or pale yellow; tops were of Micarta laminate; and tambour front panels of either ash or walnut.

Called "Action Office," the furniture was intended to be used in a private office, but components were soon adapted

In 1968, Herman Miller introduced the world's first systems furniture, Action Office 2. Made up of individual components and free-standing panels, it opened the door to a whole new way of thinking about space planning, lighting, acoustics, and color treatment (preceding pages).

PHOTO: *Herman Miller.*

for use with the free-standing panels of the increasingly popular open office, and Herman Miller is credited with introducing the first systems furniture, Action Office 2, in 1968.

Citing a shift in attitude from the production of "things" toward the management of work, office design theorist Robert Malone wrote in *Contract* magazine in 1969, "Both the 'Action Office' and the 'Office Landscape' concepts are expressions of a philosophy of work. . . . They are also commendably humane attempts to make the environment of work more workable, and less of a strain on the people using it."

A year earlier, *PA* had also acknowledged that office landscape had some long-established attitudes about work to overcome.

"In the last few decades, we have seen the fullest flowering of the cool business esthetic, powerfully advocated by such designers as SOM and the Knoll Planning Unit. . . . Only a couple of years ago, we saw what seemed the ultimate in this cool, rectilinear order, Total Design, that turned the office into a Platonic composition of official art, official plans, and official ashtray positions, implying a military academy gone esthetic. To suggest to many an executive that, for reasons of efficiency, all this must be scrapped in favor of office landscape's serpentine aisles and oddly-angled desks, with the executive himself bivouacking in their midst, is to propose abomination."

Despite the controversy, open office planning in the '60s and the systems furniture it spawned brought about the most significant changes for office interiors in the twentieth century. In terms of design, it offered a whole new way of thinking about space planning, furniture, textiles, carpeting, and color. The flexibility of systems furniture was a perfect match for the changing technology of automation. It was somewhat slow to catch on, but when it finally did in the mid-'70s, it fueled the contract furniture industry's growth for almost 20 years.

the '70s
chapter three

In 1976, when author Tom Wolfe wrote an essay about the '70s titled, "The Me Decade and the Third Great Awakening," he wasn't necessarily referring to a narcissistic, greedy, "I can get away with anything" America. Instead, he was citing what he thought was a shift from basic materialism — the accumulation of things brought on by the post-World War II economic expansion — to a higher level of luxury that was characterized by self-analyzation of one's conduct, relationships, hang-ups, or personality. According to Wolfe, this actually helped the feminist movement and ushered in the "Third Great Awakening" — of religion — in America in the '70s.

"Out of such intense concentration upon the self . . . came a feeling that was decidedly religious, binding one beaming righteous soul to the other in the name of the cause," he wrote in an article for *Life* magazine in 1979. ". . . Such was the hunger for some form of spiritual strength that any obsession was sufficient to found a faith upon: Jogging, flying, UFOs, ESP, health foods, or drug rehabilitation."

Yet if Americans did turn inward, it may have been because the age of innocence was over. The forced resignations of Vice President Spiro Agnew in 1973 because of income tax evasion and President Richard Nixon over the Watergate scandal the following year were tremendous blows to Americans' confidence in government. Formal U.S. involvement in the Vietnam War also ended in 1973, but most

Americans were too disillusioned to care. The escalation of significant terrorist attacks — up from 293 in 1970 to 1,511 in 1979 according to *New York* magazine — created worldwide concern, but generated little effective action toward protecting the innocent.

An energy crisis caused lines at the gas station and created a new desire for smaller cars. For the first time, Americans realized that resources were not limitless. They also woke up to the fact that they could not continue to pollute and trash their environment — the first Earth Day was held in 1970. Most Americans will never forget the '70s image of a tear rolling down the cheek of an old Indian chief at the sight of a polluted river and garbage-littered landscape.

Besides the environment, other movements that took hold in the '70s were gay and women's liberation.

Lasting inflation cut the dollar's value in half. A "buy now, pay later" spending spree to hedge against this inflation caused the total credit market debt to triple in the '70s. New York City's fiscal crisis was a strong indication that the ultimate welfare state was at an end. The country experienced its worst recession in 40 years, with economic growth sluggish. But, by the end of the decade, Americans were decidedly tired of material growth as the solution to economic health.

In 1976, America's 200th anniversary, Democratic candidate Jimmy Carter was elected president by a populace seeking a moral change in government to replace the tainted Republican record.

Technology had produced new "toys" for the American public to play with — eight-track tapes replaced record players; Cuisinart introduced its food processor; Sony came out with the Betamax videotape player; Texas Instruments started the pocket calculator; and Wilson replaced the wooden tennis racquet with a metal model, the T-2000. In 1977, Silicon Valley upstart Apple Computer introduced the world's first practical personal computer, the Apple II. The Concorde, Xerox machine, and direct-dial long distance telephone were also inventions of the '70s. Sports enthusiasts paid $40 for Nike running shoes and were introduced to Nautilus machines at the gym. Executives collected Pet Rocks, Trova kaleidoscopes, and Lucite cube sculptures.

STRUTTING YOUR STUFF

Disco fever swept the country, a phenomenon captured by the movie *Saturday Night Fever*, starring John Travolta. Disco spawned its own fashion cult and local clubs became the place to see and be seen. Country and western also enjoyed brief popularity — also brought to the mainstream by a Travolta film, *Urban Cowboy*.

Individuality characterized fashion in the '70s. People didn't follow fashion, they defined it for themselves by wearing hot pants and boots; battle jackets and platform shoes; bell-bottoms and bodysuits. The "Gatsby" look was popular for a time, as were pantsuits, clogs, the peasant look, Western boots, goose-down parkas and vests, the "Annie Hall" look, designer jeans, jogging suits, T-shirts with opinions, stiletto heels, and the punk look. The suit returned, and the executive woman was born.

At the movies, Americans were dazzled by the special effects of *Star Wars*; nostalgic over *American Graffiti*; fascinated by the brutality of *The Godfather*; and heartened by the gritty determination of *Rocky*. According to Tom Wolfe, Woody Allen was the "archetypal Hollywood figure of the 1970s," snubbing the Oscars, wearing his own style of "funky chic" clothing — cheap cotton plaid shirts.

At home, people turned on their television sets to watch a proliferation of sitcoms and action drama shows, such as "All in the Family," "The Jeffersons," "Charlie's Angels," "Happy Days," and "The Waltons." Alex Hailey's "Roots" was broadcast as the first-ever TV miniseries. On Broadway, theatregoers flocked to *A Chorus Line* and *Annie*. People danced to the music of Donna Summer; listened to opera greats Luciano Pavarotti and Beverly Sills; turned up the slam-bang rock 'n' roll of Kiss; and found kinship with the ballads of Bruce Springsteen and Elton John.

In 1977-78, crowds flocked to museums across the country to see the "Treasures of Tutankhamen" exhibit, which featured 55 treasures found in the tomb of King Tutankhamen, the teenage pharoh who died in 1355 B.C. America was soon engulfed in "Tut-mania," as Egyptian motifs and golden colors began to appear in jewelry, fashion, products for the home and office, and even hairdos. Comedian Steve Martin joined the movement by writing and performing a song spoofing King Tut, which became an instant hit on radio and television.

INTERNATIONAL STYLE WANES

In general, office buildings in the '70s still reflected the modernist aesthetic, but many architects were beginning to question the established architectural values of the International Style. The "black box" office buildings as a symbol of power and achievement were giving way to a new view of corporate image that emphasized individual needs.

"Even office buildings, whose facades at any rate had been a direct expression of the power and achievement of the client company — typified by works like Mies van der Rohe's Seagram Building or Roche and Dinkeloo's Ford Foundation — began to reflect in the seventies a much more equivocal attitude towards corporate power," wrote Udo Kultermann in 1980.

Yet, skyscrapers built in the '70s still reflected corporate status, as well as various architects' individuality and desire to break away from the modernist principles. Many were successful in breaking up the rectangular plan by using different shapes and changing the simple facades of office buildings through banding and reflective glass. Some examples of this include the stepped back design of the Sears Tower in Chicago, designed by SOM and completed in 1970; the dramatic pyramidal shape of the Transamerica Corporation building in San Francisco, designed by William Pereira and completed in 1972; the diagonal wedges of the Penzoil Plaza in Houston, designed by Johnson and Burgee and completed in 1975; and the chamfering of the World Trade Center in New York, designed by Minoru Yamasaki and completed in 1977.

Technocratic architecture, defined by Mary Hollingsworth as a style based on the "Brutalist approach to an undisguised expression of structure and surfaces," also appeared at the end of the '70s. Richard Rodgers's Lloyd's Building in London (1978-86) is perhaps the most vivid example. According to Hollingsworth, it "combines the space-age image of technocracy with references to early industrial architecture and the conservatories of Victorian England in its huge curved glass roof, which crowns the interior atrium."

This large office project was the first
insurance company in Columbus, OH., to build
a new building and fully landscape it with
systems furniture. Finished in 1976, different
floors were given dominant color schemes
of green, navy blue, and burgundy.

PROJECT:

Grange Insurance Companies,
Columbus, OH.

INTERIOR DESIGN:

Design Collective Incorporated.

PHOTO: *Hedrich-Blessing.*

Another big change in the mid-'70s occurred in the attitude toward the practice of architecture. Large firms, faced
with an economic recession and fewer building commissions,
turned to interior design. Most were surprised to find it to be
challenging, serious, and satisfying work. It was profitable, as
well — "in many cases more profitable than that majestic old
architecture they had been obsessed with," wrote Stanley
Abercrombie in 1982. Architects finally fell in love with interi-
or design.

OFFICE LANDSCAPING MATURES

Though it took almost 10 years to catch on, most large
corporations by the mid-'70s had incorporated an open office
format in some form or another. The *AIA Journal* reported in
1977 that by 1976, systems furniture accounted for 10 percent of the office furniture industry's annual sales, compared to
two percent in 1973. What was eventually to evolve into open
plan office design — a modified version of landscaping in
which workstations took on more of a grid format rather than
free-form flow — enjoyed ongoing controversy in the '70s.

Touted as a more humanistic approach to office design, many felt office landscaping's real success was due to its cost savings. "The economy of movable, tax-depreciable space dividers as opposed to permanent walls is such that few large companies can resist," wrote the *AIA Journal* in 1974.

Yet the open office concept was predicated on a shift in management style that was directly connected to the office environment. In discussing why John Hancock made a commitment to office landscape for its new 60-story office tower in Boston in 1971, designer Jordan A. Berman, IBD, wrote in *Contract*, "We were, in fact, dealing with an environmental planning concept that had clear potential as a managerial tool."

Similarly, the writings of Robert Probst, designer of Herman Miller's Action Office, was excerpted in the *AIA Journal* in 1974: "The egg crate concept, with rows of enclosures connected by corridors, fits an organizational behavior format already rare and certainly obsolete: a form of linear communication based on almost totally vertical organization."

Yet increasing office automation was predicted by many in the late '70s as the biggest agent of change in the office environment. How would this affect office landscaping? The *AIA Journal* stated in 1977 that increasing automation would result in a "substantial reduction in the need for papers and files and other reference materials, and of person-to-person communications in the office. And there goes one of the principal justifications for open landscape planning, namely that it enhances communication and interaction among employees."

Nevertheless, embraced by management for its efficiency, economy, and flexibility, user reaction was office landscaping's biggest problem. Lack of privacy, noise, and issues of territoriality were frequent complaints. In an attempt to create a "sense of place" for personalized work areas, Herman Miller introduced fabric options in the early '70s for its Action Office panels that featured brightly colored patterns. Called "Environmental Enrichments," the fabrics were designed by Alexander Girard and capitalized on the ecology movement by featuring bold nature motifs.

Live plants also brought the outdoors in and added green to many office landscapes. Various forms of color-coded signage, necessary to orient visitors through the maze of look-alike partitions and work areas, also was introduced to the landscape palette.

In 1977, Donald Canty reported in the *AIA Journal* that the 360,000 sq. ft. Weyerhaeuser Co. headquarters building near Tacoma, Wash., represented the largest installation of open landscaping in the U.S. to date. Designed by the San Francisco office of SOM, the project had no enclosed offices and featured the very first wood landscape system, which was designed by Knoll.

"Components of the system are of red oak (except on the fifth floor, where they are of white oak)," wrote Canty. "Dividers are surfaced in white mohair and wool weave over a padded base. Teak-finished white oak frames the glass and the core walls, which are a textured linen weave painted white."

Stating that the wood gave the Weyerhaeuser landscape a warmer feeling, Canty nonetheless was disappointed in the project's color scheme. "It is somewhat bland, however, the only bright colors being in the carpet, upholstered furniture and works of art," he wrote. "There is, in fact, talk of replacing some of the white fabric on the dividers with stronger colors."

Use of nature scenes, lighter woods, and green in office interiors came to symbolize the ecology movement of the '70s (following page).

PROJECT:

Bristol-Myers Squibb Company Headquarters and Research Facility, Lawrenceville, NJ.

INTERIOR DESIGN:

Hellmuth, Obata & Kassabaum Interiors.

PHOTO: *Barbara Martin.*

Supporting the ecology movement,
designers humanized the office by using scenes
of nature and plants.
PROJECT:
Northwestern Mutual Life Insurance Co.,
Milwaukee, WI.
INTERIOR DESIGN:
Swanke Hayden Connell.
PHOTO: *Peter Vanderwarker.*

Designers found they liked combining
lighter woods with forest green. Note the pop
art flower posters on the wall.
PROJECT:
Ernst & Young (formerly Arthur Young &
Company), Los Angeles, CA.
INTERIOR DESIGN:
Cole Martinez Curtis and Associates.
PHOTO: *Leland Lee.*

The first wood landscape furniture system
was manufactured by Knoll for
Weyerhaeuser Co. in the mid-'70s. Made with
red oak, dividers were upholstered
with white mohair and wool weave.

PROJECT:

Weyerhaeuser Co., Tacoma, WA.

ARCHITECTURE/INTERIOR DESIGN:

Skidmore, Owings & Merrill.

PHOTO: *Ezra Stoller, © ESTO.*

COLOR MOVES FROM PRIMARIES TO EARTH TONES

Although remembered for its earth tones, the early part of the decade revealed more of the same bright colors of the '60s. Color was still used in large, monochromatic expanses — in carpeting and as accents on upholstery. Red, yellow, and blue primaries lingered, but the palette definitely moved into earth tones in the middle of the decade.

In response to the growing importance of color in interiors, the Color Association of the United States (CAUS), the oldest forecasting organization in America, began producing a "home furnishings" card in 1970. Interpreted for its crossover applications for commercial design, the 1970 card showed bright greens, yellows, reds, and blues. In its evaluation of the card, CAUS observed that "materials and color have become more important than form."

Color in the Office
The '70s

Many will remember the '70s as
the decade of brown (left).
PROJECT:
Willkie Farr & Gallagher, New York.
INTERIOR DESIGN:
Swanke Hayden Connell.
PHOTO: *Otto Baitz.*

Open plan systems furniture allowed colors,
textures, and furniture components to be
intermixed for visual interest and flexibility.
PROJECT:
Pennzoil Company, Houston, TX.
INTERIOR DESIGN:
Gensler and Associates/Architects.
PHOTO: *Richard Payne.*

Long white corridor walls provided perfect

canvas for early '70s supergraphics.

PROJECT:

Cole Martinez Curtis and Associates offices.

INTERIOR DESIGN:

Cole Martinez Curtis and Associates.

PHOTO: *Leland Lee.*

Indeed, prior to the widespread use of office landscaping, designers were somewhat daring with corporate offices, integrating bold color and graphics with architectural elements against off-white or white backdrops. Leading this effort was The Space Design Group in New York, whose trademark design was, according to *Contract* magazine in 1970, the "strong architectural flavor that sets the scale of the total environment." One of the firm's principal designers, Frank Failla, was quoted as saying, "When dealing with large space, color is an effective tool to control and unify. A tremendous amount of color can be unbearably overpowering. Should we, for the sake of argument, translate all the white into color, it would be heavy, overly colored, and quite depressing."

While the use of paint, upholstery, and carpet were common methods of adding graphic color diversity to office interiors in the early '70s, artwork continued to be an important element. Updated versions of the tapestry — including appliqué hangings, banners, macramé hangings, and American Indian rugs — were a popular medium used to provide an economical means of adding color and texture to spaces.

Early Steelcase systems furniture featured

white metal trim, wood laminate tops, with

primary colored upholstery fabric (opp. page).

PHOTO: *Steelcase.*

Supergraphics provide colorful diversion
for general office workers in this 1973
project. Note the absence of systems furniture
(opp. page and right).

PROJECT:

Johns-Manville, Waterville, OH.

INTERIOR DESIGN:

The Space Design Group.

PHOTOS: *The Space Design Group.*

Visual observations of the CAUS forecasts throughout the decade show an amazingly consistent palette, with avocado greens and oranges remaining. In 1973, there was a shift from bright to more muted tones, and a brief fascination with gold as the nation went wild over King Tut. In offices, off-white yielded to beige as earth tones became dominant in the mid-'70s. Most furniture manufacturers offered few colors other than beige as finish options for the metal components of systems furniture. Some have speculated that this was because it coordinated well with the "putty" color of computer equipment. Metal chair finishes, for the most part, were either chrome or black.

Striking black and white graphics and
electrifying blue upholstery characterize this
early '70s executive office (following page).

PROJECT:

Touche-Ross, New York.

INTERIOR DESIGN:

The Space Design Group.

PHOTO: *Bernard Liebman.*

Panels provided many opportunities

for experimentation with color (below).

PROJECT:

Safeway Stores, Walnut Creek, CA.

INTERIOR DESIGN:

The Austin Company.

PHOTO COURTESEY OF: *Susan L. Wood.*

Never shy about using color, The Space Design Group was a master at integrating bold color and graphics with architectural elements. Corridor spaces are embellished with fabric-covered walls, carpet insets, and painted ceilings (page 59 and right). The lobby features a unique lighting system, lime green carpet dotted with marble planters, blue panels, and a red carpet inset that leads up to the chairman's office (page 58). A wide corridor (left) offers a glimpse of brightly upholstered chairs in perimeter offices.

PROJECT:

Johns-Manville, Denver, Col.

INTERIOR DESIGN:

The Space Design Group.

PHOTOS: *Leibman Lewis.*

ACT observed in 1990 that "as the psychological effects of color became a topic, the palette for contract interiors [in the '70s] gradually shifted to lighter, calmer, more neutral shades. . . . Beiges, off-whites, taupes, oatmeals, light browns and tans were the colors of choice." Pattern took a back seat to texture and machine-loomed fabrics with natural hand-woven looks were favored by designers. Textile companies founded in the '60s and early '70s (such as ArcCom, Coral of Chicago, and Design Tex) flourished as widespread use of systems furniture created a need for COM panel fabrics that offered more color and design options.

preference for off-white interiors, stating that it had "reached epidemic proportions."

"Architects have been traditionally conservative in the use of color," he wrote. "They have been trained to think mainly in terms of form, expressed in black, gray and white. To many of them a prejudice or timidity about color can be traced to the fact that color is likely to detract from form. Because color is more primitive in its appeal than form, a building exterior or interior designed, for example, in red or yellow, green or blue, may be judged by the average mortal more for its hue rather than its shape."

Perhaps as a prelude to the postmodern '80s, by the end of the '70s architects were starting to expand their visual and emotional vocabulary by using more color in building exteriors. Color was employed to highlight details, coordinate with the landscape, or reduce mass and volume.

Acknowledging that their observations of revised architectural expectations of color was most clearly demonstrated in building exteriors, *AIA Journal* editors wrote in 1978: ". . . recently, this is being joined by subtler investigations into the manipulation of spatial perceptions through color; color as an element of composition to activate or delineate space; the suggestion of more complicated moods."

. . . . itects, they maintained, "have been looking . . . . hoices. Not only the . . . . ly the

. . . . . . rior

. . . . . . ture of

Gray was just beginning to creep into office interiors in the late '70s.

PROJECT:

Xerox Corporation, Stamford, CN.

INTERIOR DESIGN:

Interior Space International

(acquired I S D Incorporated in 1991).

PHOTO: *Jaime Ardiles-Arce.*

the '80s
chapter four

WHO AND WHAT:

Bull market

Ronald Reagan

Working women

LBOs

Yuppies

MTV

Fax machines

Casual chic

Michael Jackson

Mazda Miata

Postmodrnism

OFFICE COLORS:

Gray

Mauve

Pastels

Neon brights

Black

When the '80s began, the country was in a recession and Ronald Reagan had just been elected to the first of two terms he would serve as president. The Dow-Jones Industrial Average was approximately 825, but would later top 2700 — the result of the greatest bull market since the Roaring '20s. During his term, Reagan policies that favored big business propelled the economy to new strengths. According to *Time* magazine, employment rose by 18 million, and median household income grew to a modest $27,000 a year, with the top 20 percent of family earnings reaching an average high of $85,000 a year by the decade's end. Housing prices in major metropolitan areas soared between 1984-1987, doubling and sometimes tripling in value within an incredibly short time span. Office towers sprang up one after another in cities across the U.S., pushing vacancy rates up, but creating ongoing construction jobs in the meantime.

Tax cuts and deregulation of industry in 1981 launched the boom, which resulted in the second longest economic expansion in U.S. history. It was an "anything goes" decade, characterized by deal makers whose creed was to get rich, spend, borrow, and enjoy. High-risk debt became more readily available through the issue of junk bonds. Corporate takeovers, leveraged buyouts, and mergers made big money and big money men. Near the end of the decade, companies began to restructure: selling off assets, getting rid of management layers, and "unbundling" conglomerates.

This economic boom was not without repercussions. Reagan policies created a huge budget deficit as America became the world's biggest debtor. Oil prices fell from $34 a barrel in 1982 to $9 in 1986, touching off a major recession in Texas. Some of Wall Street's overnight millionaires were later found to be guilty of insider trading. The stock market plunged 700 points in one day in October 1987, only to surpass its all-time high a year later. Homelessness increased as federal housing subsidies diminished and real estate prices soared. *Time* reported in 1990 that the bottom 20 percent of family earnings ended up at an average of $8,800 a year.

HAVING IT ALL

Yet despite the negative side, the '80s were a time of astonishing prosperity. Labeled by some as the "My Decade," those coming of age during the '80s were intent on having it all. Improving opportunities for women in business led to an unprecedented number of working moms. Young urban professionals, labeled "yuppies," epitomized this lifestyle through the acquisition of material wealth in the form of BMWs, Cuisinarts, VCRs, minivans, and more. Demands on their time meant that eating out two or three times a week was not unusual. At the same time, baby boomers were reaching middle age, and sociologists began to talk about the "graying of America." Being healthy was in for both young and old, with more Americans than ever taking to the streets to jog, power walk, cycle, or skate.

As usual, America's youth during the '80s got much of its inspiration from music. High-energy rock videos, sometimes shocking in their violent and sexual overtones, were suddenly viewed by millions via Music Television (MTV), whose edgy, unruly graphics set standards for popular culture. Superstars such as Michael Jackson and Madonna inspired thousands of "wanna be" imitators. Bruce Springsteen struck a patriotic chord with millions of kids as well as adults with his "Born in the U.S.A." album in 1984. In the late '80s, rap music, with its tough-talking lyrics, became the controversial urban medium. Drugs and alcohol, the sustenance of '60s and '70s rock bands, were not as cool toward the end of the decade, and many musicians started advocating to "just say no."

Technology continued to change the way Americans communicated and entertained themselves in the '80s. IBM unveiled its first PC in 1981, and Apple came out with the "user friendly" Macintosh in 1984. The availability of personal computers suddenly meant that almost every office worker had one on his or her desk — and maybe one at home, too. Scores of schoolchildren became computer literate. At work, the facsimile machine became the preferred choice of sending material; calls were answered by voice mail; and cellular phones made doing business from the freeway easy. At home, compact disk players, video camcorders, and remote controls for television became the electronic toys of choice.

Popular television shows at the beginning of the decade, such as "Dallas," "Dynasty," and "Knots Landing" presented sensational sagas of wealthy families trying to hold on to their fortunes. Interest had begun to shift back to "real people" by the end of the '80s, with shows like "Roseanne," "thirtysomething," and "The Wonder Years" at the top of the ratings chart. In the interim, Michael Mann brought us "Miami Vice," the trendy cop show that featured flashy clothes, fast cars, and rock music narration. Frugal Gourmet Jeff Smith offered Americans simple, cheerful cooking tips and David Letterman entertained them with stupid pet tricks.

The '80s also produced movies such as *Kramer vs. Kramer*, *Raiders of the Lost Ark*, *First Blood*, *ET*, *Back to the Future*, *Who Framed Roger Rabbit*, and Batman. Superstars Meryl Streep, Cher, Eddie Murphy, and Sylvester Stallone dominated the silver screen.

Every major city built a new museum or expanded an old one during the '80s. Galleries proliferated, and a growing interest in art for public spaces allowed more artists to work in tandem with architects and developers. There was a revival of the American arts and crafts movement, supported by the opening of specialized museums in cities such as New York and Chicago. Major exhibits of artifacts from India and Russia toured the country, as well as works of artists such as Van Gogh, Georgia O'Keefe, and Andy Warhol. Prices for masterpieces soared: According to *Life* magazine, a Picasso that sold for $5.8 million in 1981 went for $47.9 million in 1989.

Design as an art form experienced renewed interest. Mazda received accolades for coming up with the first good-looking production sports car, the Miata. Architects designed household items, such as dinnerware, sheets, and teapots, that soon became collectibles. The Vietnam Veterans Memorial in Washington, D.C., designed by Maya Ying Li, was powerful and controversial. The Macintosh jolted the stodgy computer industry with its sexy, stylish, trim lines.

On the fashion front, conservative elegance, donned by the decade's most popular cover girl, Britain's Princess Diana, and First Lady Nancy Reagan paved the way to a new sophistication. Casual chic emphasized the body and legs, with outfits that included shoulder pads, tights, big blazers, and baggy sweaters. Swatch introduced its first watch in 1983. Skirt lengths went up with the stock market, only to be pulled back down by thirty- and fortysomething women who didn't want to bare their thighs at work.

Black dominated couture until Christian Lacroix introduced his "pouf" dresses in 1985 with bright colors, spots, and shapes. Tapestry looks, sequins, and gilt added shimmer to evening wear. Ralph Lauren's country line brought Americans back to their roots with the "natural" look. Calvin Klein elevated ready-to-wear sports clothes to new popularity; and Chanel re-established the "power suit." By the end of the '80s, according to *Vogue* magazine, personal style took over. Black, the decade's reigning fashion color, stepped aside in favor of whites and brights.

MICHAEL GRAVES FUELS POSTMODERN CRAZE

Although office interiors in the early '80s continued on the same path as the '70s, it was the postmodern architectural movement that most profoundly impacted colors and styles overall. Some preferred to call it "ornamentalism," rationalizing that it was an evolution of modernism embellished by patterning and decoration. Although, Robert Venturi was an early proponent of this style, postmodern architecture didn't gain widespread popularity until the '80s, when his work and that of New York-based architects Robert A.M. Stern and Phillip Johnson were recognized as the "new style."

Color is applied on door jams and lighting fixtures in this early '80s project. White furnishings and walls are softened by taupe carpeting, a color that would gain popularity at the end of the decade.

PROJECT:

1st American Bank of Virginia, McLean, VA.

INTERIOR DESIGN:

The Space Design Group.

PHOTOS: *Mark Ross.*

Postmodern architecture, with its ornamentation and palette of cool pinks, greens, and gray-blues, took its cues in the '80s from the work of Michael Graves. His signature approach not only included buildings and interiors, but also furnishings, textiles, and even tabletop items (left and right).

PROJECT:

Crown American Corporate Office Building, Johnstown, PA.

ARCHITECTURE/INTERIOR DESIGN:

Michael Graves, Architect.

PHOTOS: *Tim Hursley.*

But none of these practitioners captured the public eye like Princeton architect Michael Graves. His milestone Portland Public Services Building, completed in 1983 — perhaps the most visible example of his work at the time — used large-scale ornamentation in combination with color and abstract forms to create a new architectural vocabulary. Graves's work was a successful melding of modernism and classicism. His vernacular would be translated from the exterior to the interior in showrooms he later designed for SunarHauserman in New York and Chicago; the Humana Corporation headquarters in Louisville, Ky.; and hotels for Disney in Florida.

N.Y. Times architecture critic Paul Goldberger summed up his popularity in 1982 when he wrote,

"It has thus fallen to Michael Graves to become the figure around which the public's interest in postmodernism has coalesced. Graves' work is ideally suited to such a position. It is lively, genuinely fresh, and committed both to seriousness of purpose and to ease of communication. Graves is perhaps the only architect practicing today who has managed to devise an essentially new style — to create buildings that really do not look like anyone else's and seem to speak in a new voice."

Color integrated well with postmodern

architectural elements.

PROJECT:

HBO, New York.

INTERIOR DESIGN:

Kohn Pedersen Fox Interior Architects

(KPFIA).

PHOTO: *Peter Aaron, © ESTO.*

This new style included a set of complex color patterns that was a direct association with nature. Terra cotta symbolized the earth; gray was for stone; green, the landscape; and blue as the sky. All of Graves's work — buildings, showrooms, furniture, fabrics, and even teapots — used these colors as an integral part of their design. Goldberger wrote this about Graves's interiors, "What drama Graves' rooms have comes more from the processional sequence from one of them to another than from each room's intrinsic quality. At any single point, most Graves rooms, whether round, square, or oblong, are serene and ordered, set pieces of decoration defined by color and detail more than by a dynamic sense."

Stone and buff colors were also characteristic of the postmodern palette, with gray as the dominant neutral.

PROJECT:

American Express Corporation, New York.

INTERIOR DESIGN:

Swanke Hayden Connell Architects.

PHOTO: *Wolfgang Hoyt.*

Interior designers embraced Graves's rose tones, blue greens, and grays. Soon, they were the office color palette of preference. As designers experimented with Graves's postmodern palette, they began to use more architectural details. Office spaces done in the mid- to late '80s sported new incarnations of decorative columns, pilasters, pediments, bases, and moldings. Almost every design scheme had a postmodern inclination. Other elements, such as lighting, furniture, and millwork, followed the same language. Each was a surface ripe for color.

Furniture manufacturers encouraged ornamentalism in the office by introducing pieces to support the trend. In 1983, SunarHauserman commissioned Graves to do a line of tables; The Gunlocke Co. unveiled its dramatic Utopian Collection of desks and credenzas by Wendell Castle; and Harvey Probber had a desk line called the Post Modern System. Knoll delighted the design world in 1984 with collection of playful postmodern Robert Venturi-designed chairs, tables, and sofa.

MEMPHIS—A FLASH IN THE PAN

Another popular style that had its effect on color, though brief, was the Memphis movement, which surfaced in 1981 during the Milan Furniture Fair. Led by Italian Ettore Sottsass, a group of designers staged an exhibition of "avant garde" furniture that both shocked and delighted the design community. Curious shapes, dense patterns, and bright colors characterized this furniture, giving it a bizarre, playful quality. Prototypes also included pieces by Michael Graves, Japanese architect Arata Isozaki, and Viennese architect Hans Hollein.

Its notoriety drew international attention, despite the fact that some wondered if it was really "good design." But it dominated the Milan Fair for the next two years and brought forth a new generation of Italian "counter designers." The Memphis look penetrated mass culture in the U.S. and abroad, bringing crazy patterns and wild colors to fashion, graphics, and furniture. TV's sensational cop show, "Miami Vice," nonchalantly blended Memphis style with Latino chic in its sets and scenes. Always in vogue, Hollywood filled the house of Bette Midler's character in the 1986 movie, *Ruthless People*, with Memphis furniture.

Color in the Office

The '80s

Perhaps the extreme of postmodernism

furniture was a line designed by

Wendell Castle for The Gunlocke Company.

PHOTO: *The Gunlocke Company.*

By the mid-'80s, few offices were

designed without gray.

PROJECT:

Prudential Bache Securities, New York.

INTERIOR DESIGN:

Swanke Hayden Connell Architects.

PHOTO: *Dan Cornish.*

But it never gained total public acceptance. Memphis furniture was just too wacky and too expensive for upper-middle-class taste. As for design, color forecasters predicted that neon brights would invade interiors at the height of Memphis's popularity in 1984. This never really happened in the office, save a few "spots" of hot colors woven into textiles and floor-covering. But it did serve as inspiration for new patterns and shapes in textiles, furniture, and materials. And even a few progressive clients asked for Memphis-style office interiors.

Besides Memphis, bright colors got another boost from the graphics created for the 1984 Summer Olympic Games in Los Angeles. Developed by Sussman/Prejza & Co. in collaboration with The Jerde Partnership, the Games' brilliant color program was dubbed "Festive Federal" for its spirited attitude. Principal Deborah Sussman described the palette in 1984 to *Interiors* magazine as one that ". . . breaks away from all the schemes that evolved through the 1970s. The key color is magenta, with vermillion, aqua, and chrome yellow representing the Southern California spirit. And lighter 'Mediterranean' colors are occasionally used in large backgrounds. . . ."

Knoll's homage to the postmodern

movement was a line of seating introduced in

1984 designed by Robert Venturi (opp. page).

PHOTO: *Knoll Group.*

The curious shapes, dense patterns, and
bright colors of Memphis furniture both shocked
and delighted the design community.
PHOTO COURTESY OF: *Urban Architecture.*

Apple Computer's offices reflect its
bold and aggressive corporate identity. Bright
colors, bold shapes, and diverse patterns seem
to have Memphis roots (opp. page).

PROJECT:

Apple Computer, Stevens Creek, CA.

INTERIOR DESIGN:

Gensler and Associates / Architects.

PHOTO: *Peter Aaron,* © ESTO.

MAUVE RULES

But the real color story of the '80s revolves around mauve and gray, whose popularity was propelled by the postmodern movement. An examination of Color Association of the United States (CAUS) forecasts for interiors during the decade reveals a saturated palette in 1981, followed by a series of muted, grayed-out palettes with variations of deep reds, dark blues, desert browns, tawny taupes, and blue-greens. Gray makes its first appearance as an individual grouping of colors on the board in the 1982-83 forecast. Just one year later, in 1983-84, the entire palette is under the gray influence, with the strongest families still blue, green, and rosy-reds. Fashion colors celadon and olive also show up at this time, along with metallic silver, suggested as an accent in weaving — the first hint of an interest in luster.

Neon brights characterized casual fashion in the mid-'80s. In offices, it was used mostly for accent, but some did like it "hot."

PROJECT:

Amsted Industries, Chicago, IL.

INTERIOR DESIGN:

Swanke Hayden Connell Architects.

PHOTO: *Abby Sadin.*

A late '80s Apple project is energized with pattern, materials, and primaries (preceding pages).

PROJECT:

Apple De Anza 3, Cupertino, CA.

INTERIOR DESIGN:

Gensler and Associates/Architects.

PHOTO: *Marco Lorenzetti, Hedrich-Blessing.*

Muted, soft shades dominated the 1984-85 forecast, which was described by CAUS as a "counterbalance to the turmoil of our time. . . . Repose, quiet and comfort, important psychological factors, are reflected in this presentation's cool tonalities." Dusty rose shades evolve from mauve in this palette; neutrals and off-whites are tinted with yellow, green, or pink; greens and celadon are muted; and grays are tinged with blue. The following year, CAUS cites a "major move towards blue," but dusty roses and coral pinks — the descendants of mauve — maintain importance. The same tinted off-whites appear, with more yellow influence. Black materializes as a foil, but its strength as an interiors color is underestimated by the CAUS forecasters.

Then, just as designers were pleading "no more mauve," the palette brightened in 1986-87, perhaps a reflection of the optimistic social outlook generated by the '84 Olympic Games and presidential campaign. There seemed to be a new openness to using color. Overall, CAUS predicted a move "toward

Color can often give a low-budget project
vitality. Here, primaries symbolize the colors of
Houston Transit Authority's buses, while the
dark carpet represents the transitways.

PROJECT:

Metropolitan Transit Authority, Houston, TX.

INTERIOR DESIGN:

Gensler and Associates/Architects.

PHOTO: *Nick Merrick, Hedrich-Blessing.*

clear hues and stronger multicolored harmonies of saturated colors." "More is more," CAUS Associate Director Margaret Walch told *Contract* magazine in January 1985. "Observe the street scenes. . . . Color combinations are much wilder — green and blue hair, an assortment of flashy jewelry, clothes, and accessories." Deep reds set a dominant direction in this color board, with dusty roses shifting to beige or blue variations. Brilliant blues and bright accents of orange, yellow, violet, and jade corresponded with fashion trends. There is a remarkable similarity between the 1986-87 forecast colors and a Van Gogh exhibit that toured the country in 1984 showing off the artist's luminous yellows, oranges, blues, and reds.

However, 1986-87 was probably the peak of bright colors in contract color forecasts. Throughout the rest of the '80s, there was a shift from brighter shades to muted pastels and neutrals that were lighter than the earlier grayed-out palettes. Purple was a late-'80s fashion color that showed up in contract interiors in gentler shades of eggplant. Teal was another strong fashion color that tended to shine at furniture shows, but when actually used in offices, was much more tame. By the end of the decade, taupes began to take over from gray as the standard neutral. That '70s outcast — brown — was once again acceptable in new softer shades. Chartreuse was a fashion hit, but not really a color for the office, unless one was wearing it. Reds, so dominant in the '80s, changed from mauve and dusty rose to coral and melon, with burgundy holding its own as a deep red. Golden Southwest oranges, reds, yellows, and browns also gained popularity — though probably more in residential design than contract.

And black cannot be overlooked as a serious color in the '80s. Designers used more black in interiors in the late '80s than ever before — perhaps as a reaction to the postmodern colors so dominant in the early part of the decade. Black on black became a popular urban fashion combination, a symbol of luxury, sophistication, and power. In interiors, however, the timeless nature of black created a strong image. It compliments light or dark wood and highlights the intensity of other colors when used as an accent or heavy surface color. Even textiles took on a new sophistication in the late '80s by incorporating black and metallic accents. Yet the degree to which

The colors and cultural associations of Old Texas reflect the Hispanic heritage of a Houston law firm's partners.

PROJECT:

Offices of Frank Herrera, San Antonio, TX.

INTERIOR DESIGN:

Ford Powell & Carson Inc.

PHOTO: *Hickey-Robertson.*

Colorful and bold, the exuberant design of
this southwest office is comfortable for both
staff and clients (left and below).

PROJECT:

Offices of Frank Herrera, San Antonio, TX.

INTERIOR DESIGN:

Ford Powell & Carson Inc.

PHOTOS: *Hickey-Robertson.*

black was used in office interiors probably varied by region, especially in the South and Southwest where the light quality is different.

A DESIRE FOR DETAIL

As designers began to use more complex color patterns in office interiors, they also developed a desire for detail. Spawned in part by the ornamentalism of the postmodern movement, this desire was carried through in patterns, textures, and reflective surfaces in almost every element specified. Systems furniture manufacturers supported this trend by overhauling their fabric and finish programs.

With the aid of the computer in production as well as styling, textile designers began weaving more intricate jacquards, mixing colors and creating motifs with both visual and tactile texture. According to the Association for Contract Textiles (ACT), small-scale geometric patterns emerged, and later gave way to "larger, more fluid designs." Breakthrough designs using color and pattern are credited to Michael Graves's postmodern textile collection for SunarHauserman and Orlando Diaz Azcuy's sophisticated neutrals for HBF.

"The Post Modern passion for ornament and decoration and the reworking of traditional themes and motifs continued to exert an influence," ACT wrote in 1990. Examples of this were abstract interpretation of artists such as Paul Klee, M.C. Escher, and Gaudi. The functional design and purity of form characteristic of the Vienna school was also reinterpreted into textiles and furniture detailing. Shiny fabrics introduced in the late 80s seemed to change color, depending on the direction from which they were viewed. Tapestry and floral patterns brought a new elegance to the office.

Likewise, carpet mills offered more possibilities for pattern and color on the floor in the '80s. Designers were able to create custom designs and use carpet tiles to do borders and special motifs underfoot. "Graffiti" patterns at first glance appeared to only have one or two shades in them, but at close examination revealed six or seven different colored yarns.

Faux finishes were also big in the '80s. Plastic laminate producers created patterns that simulated marble and stone so well they could fool even the most trained eye. These were

Black and white make a sophisticated statement while enhancing the light quality of this southern Florida office (opp. page).

PROJECT:

Capital Bank, Miami, FL.

INTERIOR DESIGN:

Gensler and Associates, Architects.

PHOTO: *Nick Merrick, Hedrich-Blessing.*

Details were important to designers in the '80s. A sophisticated palette of off white, light woods, and black accents is used in the project on the preceding pages. Artwork provides the rest of the color spectrum and livens up what otherwise would be a bland palette.

PROJECT:

Whitman Corporation, Chicago, IL.

INTERIOR DESIGN:

LSH/Hague-Richards Associates,
a division of Loebl Schlossman and Hackl.

PHOTO: *David Clifton.*

Visually rich materials and neutral colors provide a simply furnished reception area with a minimalist elegance in this late '80s design (right).

PROJECT:

Tokai Bank, Chicago, IL.

INTERIOR DESIGN:

Perkins & Will.

PHOTO: *Marco Lorenzetti, Hedrich-Blessing.*

Color in the Office
The '80s

Designers began to mix styles, reflecting
an interest in postmodern, neoclassical, and the
arts & crafts movement.
PROJECT:
Carrington Coleman, Dallas, TX.
INTERIOR DESIGN:
Interior Space International
(acquired I S D in 1991).
PHOTO: *Charles McGrath.*

used on tabletops, work surfaces, and even as wallcovering. In addition, paint was widely used to imitate stone, as well as the popular patinaed copper look.

The influx of European-designed lighting fixtures into the American market offered designers more options for illuminating office spaces than ever before. Techniques, such as washing walls with colored gels, were used to create interesting palettes and sensations. Halogen lamps and luminaires with improved color rendition made interiors sparkle. Wall sconces and other indirect lighting sources provided a sense of drama and decoration.

In the latter half of the decade, postmodern encouraged a return to neoclassical, but the palette remained the same.

PROJECT:

The Equitable Insurance Company of America, New York.

INTERIOR DESIGN:

Kohn Pedersen Fox Interior Architects(KPFIA).

PHOTO: *Paul Warchol.*

Reflected light is a technique designers began

to use in the late '80s to create color.

PROJECT: **IBM Building 15, San Jose, CA.**

INTERIOR DESIGN:

Gensler and Associates/Architects.

PHOTO: *Peter Aaron, © ESTO.*

Exposing raw space was also a favorite design

approach in the '80s. By the end

of the decade, designers were beginning to

combine different materials (preceding pages).

PROJECT:

Silicon Graphics, Mountain View, CA.

INTERIOR DESIGN:

STUDIOS Architecture.

PHOTO: *Colin McRae.*

GOING FULL CIRCLE

This quest for detail certainly led designers back to the beginning of the twentieth century. Much attention in the '80s was focused on early 1900s furniture designed by Charles Rennie Mackintosh, Joseph Hoffman, and Frank Lloyd Wright. Even the roots of Memphis furniture are in the earlier Secession, DeStijl, and Bauhaus movements. The "Boldist" style furniture presented by Massimo Isho Ghini at the 1987 Milan Furniture Fair championed the curve and reminded one of the speed-shaped, streamlined silhouette of modern ships, airplanes, and bridges of the '50s.

Gensler's approach to office design in the '80s
was classic, crisp, and very elegant (right).
PROJECT:
O'Melveny & Meyers, San Francisco, CA.
INTERIOR DESIGN:
Gensler and Associates Architects.
PHOTO: *Jon Lee, Hedrich-Blessing.*

A softened palette accentuates form
in the project on the preceding page. Lighting
helps create the atmosphere.
PROJECT:
Apple Computer, New York.
INTERIOR DESIGN:
STUDIOS Architecture.
PHOTO: *Paul Warchol.*

Textile designers, drawing inspiration from earlier artists, cultures, and design movements, found new ways to reinterpret the old. By the end of the decade, the soft postmodern colors were replaced by richly saturated "jewel tones," such as in the striking designs of newcomer Deepa Textiles. For many clients, preserving the past rather than creating the future became important, thus paving the way for a renewed interest in restoration and renovation. Designers and architects rehabbing and retrofitting older buildings into offices began to utilize many original elements as a part of the overall design scheme.

By the late '80s, neo-classicism succeeded postmodernism as the "new" design style. Throughout the decade, however, traditional interiors never seemed to go out of vogue, especially for the financial and legal sector. A revival of the Palladian-inspired Jeffersonian style in the mid-'80s surely signaled a return to the classics. Overall, the executive's office became more residential, with rich — and often updated — traditional looks taking the place of stark modernism.

Stark modernism — that which is associated with the International Style — was not without its followers in the '80s. Many offices designed in the '60s and '70s were updated with '80s colors and materials, retaining their International Style flavor through use of limited color palettes, hard edges, and clear planes. Furniture classics by Mies van der Rohe, Le Corbusier, and Marcel Breuer offered an air of timeless elegance to lobbies. Deconstructivism, another form of modernism pioneered by architects Peter Eisenman and Frank Gehry, also surfaced in the '80s. Characterized by hard metallic edges with crisp lines and strong geometrics, this style brought forth a new experimentation with industrial materials. It was not a style, however, that adapted well to office interiors — mostly it was used for showrooms, restaurants, and retail shops.

In the final analysis, office color and design trends in the '80s clearly reflect a shift to complexity and an awakening of the senses, perhaps in response to the hard, cold edges of an increasingly high tech society. Buoyed by a healthy economy, companies realized that there were tremendous growth opportunities. A 60-hour work week was not unusual for those who wanted to get ahead. Employers demanded it and young exec-

The trend to spend was reflected in the executive offices of corporate America. "Home Sweet Home" for many was the office.

PROJECT:

Quaker Oats, Chicago, IL.

INTERIOR DESIGN:

Griswold, Heckel & Kelly Associates, Inc.

PHOTO: *Judy Slagle.*

utives accepted it as part of their success regimen. For many, the office truly became a second home. It is no wonder then that in the late '80s, the role of design matured from more or less a pure aesthetic function to one that promoted health, well-being, and productivity in the working environment.

current and future directions
chapter five

The '80s definitely brought about a new sophistication to how color was used in the office. Unlimited budgets — a product of the spendthrift '80s — allowed for generous use of a rich palette of expensive and unusual fabrics, finishes, and materials. A new conservatism, fueled by a nationwide recession in the early '90s, initiated a new sensitivity to office design — one that is defined by creative use of less expensive fabrics, finishes, and materials.

This new "materiality" emphasizes the inherent texture and color of these materials. Attention to quality, detail, and cost without sacrifice to design has become an appropriate solution in times of economic downturn. Labeled as "budget" design in the '80s, it is the sensible approach to architecture and design in the '90s.

Though it may look somewhat industrial, this new design approach is a regeneration of modernism with a different color sensibility. "Today's minimalism is a kinder, gentler abstraction than that of decades past, softened by polychromatic palettes and sensuous textures," wrote the editors of *Architecture* magazine in 1992.

Those architects who never abandoned modernism are also finding that '90s budgets require new thinking about form and function. Robert Siegel, partner in the New York firm of Gwathmey Siegel, explained to *Architecture* in 1992 why they chose to use color so definitively in the Disney Contemporary

One architect's version of the new "materiality" is expressed through color variations that "play" against the roughness of stucco walls (above and opp. page).

PROJECT:

Shinko Management Offices,
Beverly Hills, CA.

ARCHITECTURE/INTERIOR DESIGN:

David Kellen, Architect.

PHOTOS: *Roland Bishop.*

Resort meeting facility in Lake Buena Vista, Fla. "When you really have no materiality, like stone or wood or steel or any of that good stuff that comes with its own color, color becomes one of the few ways within a budget-driven project to make hierarchies. This whole project became one of how color and texture would help make spaces more interesting, create background and foreground, and enhance scale issues. Color was fundamental."

This translates to a more subtle, sophisticated form of color in office interiors through creative use of space and light (both natural and artificial). Painted and textured surfaces

reflect understated color that often changes during the course of the day as the light varies. Most important is that color in the office no longer makes an outright design statement (such as this is the RED floor; this is the BLUE floor); rather it is the link between the details that creates a sense of place.

Use of color to create a sense of "place" rather than merely as form is a trend of the '90s. Cut-outs in walls of this Manhattan office reception area are lit by colored lights and reflected sunlight, energizing the space and providing abstract views to spaces beyond (above and opp. page).

PROJECT:

D.E. Shaw & Company, New York.

ARCHITECTURE/INTERIOR DESIGN:

Steven Holl Architects.

PHOTOS: *Paul Warchol.*

CONCERN FOR THE ENVIRONMENT

Tough economic times inevitably cause people to get back to basics and take stock in what they have. Faced with global warming, polluted air, dirty water, and mounting trash, Americans came to the conclusion that it was important to take steps to preserve the Earth's resources. "Reduce, reuse, and recycle" became the mantra of environmentally conscious citizens in the early '90s as the whole country almost overnight turned "green."

Use of recycled materials, nontropical woods, and energy-saving measures is socially conscious design for the '90s. It's also good business. By employing these techniques,

designers can save clients money and also save the environment.

Faux finishes have become a logical alternative for those designers seeking to preserve the environment and economize, yet still use natural materials in office interiors. This has opened up a rich palette of color choices for interiors. New technologies make it possible for manufacturers to offer simulated wood, marble, and stone in a wide range of hues. In turn, painting techniques have reached a new level of popularity and sophistication.

Understanding the science of color can also conserve resources. To maximize both natural and artificial light in the National Audubon Society's headquarters in New York, the Croxton Collaborative's design team chose colors with high reflectance values for finishes on systems furniture and surfaces. The building has been praised as one of the first energy efficient, ecologically sound, and environmentally safe interiors.

This new conservatism has also translated into a desire for longevity in color palettes. While not always subject to fads as other types of interiors, office design in the '90s emphasizes midtone earth specific neutrals — a saturated, clearer, softer, deeper color mix. The rich, dark colors of the 1994-95 Color Association of the United States Interiors forecast reflect the pared-down '90s where "obsolescence has become obsolete."

COLOR CHOICES: IT'S MORE THAN JUST BEING GREEN

With the greening of interior design, color choices do not translate into mere aesthetics to support a design approach. There is growing interest in how color affects the health and well-being of people in the work place and, ultimately, their productivity. Studies conducted by the Buffalo Organization for Social and Technical Innovation (BOSTI) have proven that the office environment can measurably affect job performance, job satisfaction, and ease and quality of communication. BOSTI's research centered around 18 facets of office design — things such as physical enclosure, aesthetics, privacy, furniture, status communication, temperature control, lighting, etc.

Unfortunately, BOSTI's research did not measure the affect of color on office workers. In fact, very little recent or conclusive research on human response to color in any type of

Color becomes an experience for those passing through this split-hued corridor (opp. page).

PROJECT:

Computer Associates. Houston, TX.

INTERIOR DESIGN:

CRSS Architects, Inc.

PHOTO: *Charles McGrath.*

environment exists. It's true that many books have been written on color psychology. However, most document only the few well-known, but dated, color studies and draw common-sense conclusions about how to use color.

For example, studies have shown that red, which is a warm color, causes the heart rate to increase; and blue, which is a cool color, causes it to decrease. Consider how workers must have been affected by the monochromatic expanses of primary colors and high light levels of office spaces of the '60s and early '70s. What would it be like to sit facing a bright red wall all day? Or be cooped up in a blue cubicle?

The simple answer is that designers should not use certain colors for areas in which the known response is not desired. But with today's sophisticated combinations, human response to color may not be able to be so precisely measured or controlled.

A study being conducted by Dr. Nancy Kwallek at the University of Texas at Austin is one of the first to research the effects of color upon office workers. Sponsored by the Institute of Business Designers'(IBD) Foundation with the support of BASF Corporation and Interface, the study is based on evaluations of subjects doing clerical work in one of three enclosed offices of different colors.

In an article written for *Record*, the Interior Design Educators Council newsletter, Dr. Kwallek stated that the research goals of the study are to:

1) evaluate worker productivity and mood in an office that simulates the interior color and lighting of a NASA space module ("NASA white");

2) compare workers' reactions to an office painted in NASA white with offices of other scientifically measured and designed color schemes;

3) gather data on perceived spaciousness and color preference;

4) recommend colors and lighting for space modules; and

5) establish a color database for designers and manufacturers to utilize in selecting appropriate materials and finishes for products and design schemes for interior environments.

"My study is based on the theory that value (lightness or darkness of a color) and saturation (brightness or dullness) are the salient characteristics in human response to color," she wrote. "Predictions were that workers would perform better, feel better, and experience more spaciousness in the office where the hue of the largest surface area was of high value and low chroma; the second largest area was of medium value and medium chroma; and the trim of low value and high chroma."

In Dr. Kwallek's study, three 8- by 11-ft. rooms were painted in different color schemes to simulate pleasant/ unpleasant and productive/nonproductive work environments. Office One is the NASA white room; Office Two's largest area is painted in bright red with medium blue-green on the lower third of the walls and pale pink for trim; and Office Three's largest area is painted in light acqua with medium red on the lower third of the walls and turquoise for trim. All three have a fluorescent light source that has a color rendering index of 90 (sunlight is 100) and projects approximately 60 foot-candles of light over the desk work surface. Ninety office workers spent four days working in one of the three test offices.

Preliminary findings indicate that by the end of the third day, workers in the predominantly red office reported significantly less vigor than the workers in the NASA white office. At the end of the fourth day, workers in the predominantly light aqua office reported less depression when compared to those in the NASA white office.

Prior to running the experiment, all workers were tested for their sensitivity to environmental factors and changes. Dr. Kwallek found that, on the average, environmentally sensitive individuals were more accurate in proofreading when they were in the predominantly aqua office as opposed to the red one. Conversely, those who easily screen environmental stimuli were more accurate in the predominately red office than in the aqua one.

These very controlled environments are unlike most offices of today, yet legitimate scientific research cannot be done unless there is a controlled environment. Dr. Kwallek's research suggests, however, that color selection based on personality types may be useful in affecting individual performance.

Whether intentional or not, a richly hued accent wall with mottled blues, greens, and purples contributes to the full-spectrum color quality of this office. It also links the space's private office, open plan area, and common use function "zones."

PROJECT:

Ivy Hill Corporation, New York.

INTERIOR DESIGN:

The Phillips Jansen Group.

PHOTO: *Norman McGrath.*

Other approaches to color psychology link the value of color to light. When Sir Isaac Newton passed a beam of light through a prism in the seventeenth century, he discovered the seven visible colors of the spectrum. From that, modern color authorities know that color is light, for color is actually produced by light reflecting off surfaces that contain one or all of the colors of the spectrum.

Humans have a biological need for light; and its healing power is the subject of intensive research studies and experiments throughout the world. In 1991, $15.5 million was spent in the U.S. by the National Institute of Mental Health on light therapy experiments. Light therapy has been successful in treating a clinical form of depression called seasonal affective disorder (SAD), as well as insomnia and infertility. NASA uses a premission light therapy regimen to help shuttle astronauts expected to work at night stay alert.

So it makes sense that color, since it is light, also has positive effects on humans. In many office interiors, the absence of natural light is simulated by full-spectrum lighting. A full-spectrum color palette for furnishings, surfaces, and accessories may also be a way to enhance the quality of the environment.

HOW WE WORK

The changing nature of work has always, and will continue, to affect how offices are designed. This will be perhaps the biggest impact upon color choices for the future work place. In a speech at NeoCon92, the office furniture exposition and conference held annually at The Merchandise Mart in Chicago, BOSTI's president Michael Brill observed that the organizational structure has become more project-based, more customer-focused, and more agile.

According to Brill, this has led to the "deconstruction" of organizations into smaller work units. Office buildings will be dispersed in locations away from the urban downtowns; there will be greater variety in the character of office buildings; less space will be needed; and companies will want to utilize existing space. Citing "workforce nomads" who will move from space to space as needed, he predicts the demise of the panel system in favor of fixed construction with flexibility to accommodate individual needs.

In experimenting with new forms of office furniture and design, Steelcase has identified the new breed of worker as the "knowledge worker" — a person who in the daily performance of their job has as their primary function to analyze, create, decide, collaborate, and act on information as their fundamental raw material. Noting that "successful companies base their business on an awareness of the critical forces that affect them — political, economic, demographic, social, and technological forces," Steelcase has also devised a formula for "organizational health." This holistic approach factors in all the elements that will affect the performance and strength of a department or company, including people, technology, work process, and architectural place.

According to Herman Miller, color and form can help offset the tools of the modern worker, as exhibited in this "Office Concept of the Future" at NEOCON '91.

PHOTO: *Herman Miller.*

Herman Miller has also experimented with new office furniture concepts, suggesting the idea of the "office of the moment," a work place that does not belong to anyone in particular, but offers personal control with colors and forms that offset the technical tools of the modern worker. In an effort to promote the design of more humane work spaces, the company is also testing an interactive computer program called "The Negotiable Environment" that interprets the personality type of an employee and matches it with an appropriate office space. Factors such as storage, display surfaces, open or closed work spaces, and shape of furniture are taken into account. Perhaps Dr. Kwallek's findings will encourage the programmers to also consider color as a legitimate option.

Given the rapid advances in technology some believe that the office of the future may be the home. "The logical extension of the wired-together workplace is that we don't need to come to the office at all," wrote James S. Russell in *Architectural Record* in June 1992. Others talk about the virtual office — the "work where you are" concept made possible by laptop or palm held computers.

Yet the social forces that have always brought workers together may be diminished if there is no office to go to. This is why office furniture manufacturers such as Steelcase and Herman Miller are exploring how these new ways of working can be adapted into the office environment. They are finding out that their corporate clients are not so adverse to change, if it means happier workers. "Companies and institutions recognize that the structure of interaction isn't always important as long as it happens," wrote Russell.

INTO THE FUTURE

Whatever the organization of the interior of the future, it is clear that color will always play an important aesthetic, if not dynamic, role in the design of the work place. Expect more research on and debate over the therapeutic qualities of color and how it can be applied to all environments, including spacecraft. New technologies will be developed that allow pigments and dyes, when applied to certain surfaces, to actually change color during the course of the day. Lighting design will also continue to change and evolve, allowing for even more sophisticated uses of color.

In addition, cultural, social, and economic forces will continue to impact color preferences. Fine art will remain an important source of color inspiration. Because the color lines between fashion, residential, and commercial design are blurring, a universal approach to color selection will be warranted.

Most of all, it is important to learn from the past and recognize that, despite all the forecasts and trends, there are no "new" colors — just new ways of looking at color, thinking about color, and combining color. Real breakthroughs will occur when those selecting color get past aesthetics and begin to think about color in terms of its effect on human performance. Communicating that concept to the client is perhaps the most important step interior designers can take to ensure their future success.

references

Introduction

Klein, Judy Graf. 1982. *The Office Book.* New York, NY: Facts on File.

Chapter 1

American Fabrics, Design and Color Quorum. Winter 1948. Vol. 5: 123-5.

Architectural Record. June 1952: 136.

Association of Contract Textiles. (Exhibit brochure, June 1990.) A Visual History of Contract Textiles: 1950-1990. Chicago, IL: NEOCON, The Merchandise Mart.

Brown, Susan, ed.(Catalogue brochure, October 1985.) Alexander Girard Designs: Fabrics and Furniture. University of Minnesota, St. Paul, MN: Herman Miller, Inc.

Caplan, Ralph. 1976. *The Design of Herman Miller.* New York, NY: Whitney Library of Design.

Design Quarterly 98/99. 1975. Nelson, Eames, Girard, Probst: The Design Process at Herman Miller. Minneapolis, MN: Walker Art Center.

Hollingsworth, Mary. 1988. *Architecture of the 20th Century.* New York, NY: Exeter Books.

Interior Design. Maria Bergson. December 1990. Vol. 61: 110.

Interiors. Modern Doesn't Pay, or Does It? March 1946. Vol. 105: 66-75.

Klein, Judy Graf. 1982. *The Office Book.* New York, NY: Facts on File.

Larsen, Jack Lenor. 1983. Chapter written for "Design Since 1945." Philadelphia, PA: The Philadelphia Museum of Art.

Larrabee, Eric, and Vignelli, Massimo. 1990. *Knoll Design.* Third Printing. New York, NY: Harry N. Abrams.

Life. December 28, 1959. Vol. 47: 36

Pearce, Christopher. 1990. *Fifties Source Book.* Secaucus, NJ: Chartwell Books.

Progressive Architecture. December 1954. Vol. 35: 138.

Progressive Architecture. January 1958. Vol. 39: 134.

Chapter 2

American Fabrics. Textiles and Contemporary Architecture. Summer 1961. No. 53: 66.

Anderson, John. Office Furniture.

Contract. April 1963. Vol. 5: 30-41.

Association of Contract Textiles. (Exhibit brochure, June 1990) A Visual History of Contract Textiles: 1950-1990. Chicago, IL: NEOCON, The Merchandise Mart.

Birren, Faber. Color: The practical, profit-and-loss aspects of color as it affects planning for group situations. *Contract.* November 1960. Vol. 1: 50-51.

Contract. November 1960. Vol. 1: 25.

Contract. Our Washington Report. February 1966. Vol. 7: 14-15.

Hollingsworth, Mary. 1988. *Architecture of the 20th Century.* New York, NY: Exeter Books.

Interiors. October 1960. Vol. 72: 140-141; 147.

Interiors. January 1964. Vol. 76: 82-84.

Interiors. December 1964. Vol. 76: 83-87.

Larrabee, Eric and Vignelli, Massimo. 1990. *Knoll Design.* Third Printing. New York, NY: Harry N. Abrams.

Life. December 26, 1969. Vol. 67: 8-9.

Malone, Robert. Onward and upward to the pushbutton office. *Contract.* April 1969. Vol. 10: 94-100.

Progressive Architecture. July 1963. Vol. 44: 130-133.

Progressive Architecture. October 1968. Vol. 49: 148-149.

Venturi, Robert. 1966. *Complexity and Contradiction in Architecture.* New York, NY. Museum of Modern Art.

Chapter 3

Abercrombie, Stanley. Interior Design: Architecture's Brave New World? *Interior Design.* April 1982. Vol. 53: 210-211.

AIA Journal. Landscaping: Idea to Industry in Ten Years. October 1974. Vol. 62: 46-47; 82.

AIA Journal. The Pros and Cons and Future Prospects of Open Landscaping. July 1977. Vol. 66: 46-47; 82.

AIA Journal. The Re-Emergence of Color as a Design Tool. October 1978. Vol. 67: 41-45.

Association of Contract Textiles. (Exhibit brochure, June 1990) A Visual History of Contract Textiles: 1950-1990. Chicago, IL: NEOCON, The Merchandise Mart.

Birren, Faber. The Off-White Epidemic: A Call for A Reconsideration of Color. *AIA Journal.* July 1977. Vol. 66: 66.

Color Association of the U.S. Home Furnishings Forecast. 1970. New York, NY.

Contract. Benton & Bowles: How Space Design Group Changed an Image-Maker's Image. May 1970. Vol. 9.

Contract. 60-Story John Hancock Tower Commits to Office Landscape. April 1971. Vol. 12.

Canty, Donald. Evaluation of an Open Office Landscape: Wyerhawuser Co. *AIA Journal.* July 1977. Vol. 66: 40-45.

Esquire. Tom Wolfe's Seventies. December 1979. Vol. 92: 36-48.

Hollingsworth, Mary. 1988. *Architecture of the 20th Century.* New York, NY: Exeter Books.

Kultermann, Udo. 1980. *Architecture in the Seventies.* New York, NY: Architectural Book Publishing Company. 1-2.

Life. Ten Years. December 1979. Vol. 2.

Miller, Nory. Color in Architecture. *AIA Journal.* October 1978. Vol. 67: 39.

New York Magazine. The Seventies and How We Got Away With It. December 31, 1979/January 7, 1980. Vol. 13: 34-39.

Wolfe, Tom. 1976. *Mauve Gloves and Madmen, Clutter and Vine.* New York, NY: Farmer, Straus & Giroux.

Chapter 4

Association of Contract Textiles. (Exhibit brochure, June 1990) A Visual History of Contract Textiles: 1950-1990. Chicago, IL: NEOCON, The Merchandise Mart.

Color Association of the U.S. Interiors Forecast 1981. Issued in October 1979. New York, NY.

Color Association of the U.S. Interiors Forecast 1982-83. Issued in October 1980. New York, NY.

Color Association of the U.S. Interiors Forecast 1983-84. Issued in October 1981. New York, NY.

Color Association of the U.S. Interiors Forecast 1984-85. Issued in October 1982. New York, NY.

Color Association of the U.S. Interiors Forecast 1986-87. Issued in October 1984. New York, NY.

Goldberger, Paul. 1983. *On the Rise: Architecture & Design in a Postmodern Age.* New York, NY: Times Publishing.

Life. Fall 1989. Vol. 12: 37.

Marberry, Sara. Dominant Reds Set Bright Color Outlook for 1986-'87. *Contract.* January

1985. Vol. 27: 198-201.

Narin, Janet. Olympic Designs. *Interiors.* February 1984. Vol. 96: 104-105.

Time. Freed from Greed? January 1, 1990. Vol. 135: 76-104.

Vogue. January 1990. Vol. 180: 214.

Chapter 5

Architecture. Color and Materials. January 1992. Vol. 81: 33.

Architecture. Beyond Convention. January 1992. Vol. 81: 62-69.

Brill, M., with Margulis, S., Konar E., and BOSTI. Using Office Design to Increase Productivity. *Workplace Design & Production*, Buffalo, NY. Vol. 1, 1984; Vol. 2, 1985.

Color Association of the U.S. Interiors Forecast 1994-95. Issued in October 1992. New York, NY.

Interiors. Finding the Right Fit: A new computer program from Herman Miller matches people with offices. March 1992. Vol. 104: 52-55.

Interior Design. National Audubon Society. August 1991. Vol. 62: 93-97.

Interior Design Show Daily. Brill Deconstructs Tyranny of Geometry. June 10, 1992: 1.

Kwallek, Nancy. Color Research in Interior Design. *Record*, the newsletter of the Interior Design Educators Council. Winter 1992: 3.

Russell, James S. The New Workplace. *Architectural Record*, June 1992. Vol. 180: 70-75.

Steelcase. 1992. Brochure printed for NeoCon92. Chicago, IL: The Merchandise Mart.

index